Legends *of* Animation

Tex
Avery

Legends of Animation

Tex Avery:
Hollywood's Master of Screwball Cartoons

Walt Disney:
The Mouse that Roared

Matt Groening:
From Spitballs to Springfield

William Hanna and Joseph Barbera:
The Sultans of Saturday Morning

Legends *of* Animation

Tex
Avery

Hollywood's Master of Screwball Cartoons

Jeff Lenburg

CHELSEA HOUSE
An Infobase Learning Company

Tex Avery: Hollywood's Master of Screwball Cartoons

Chelsea House
An Infobase Learning Company
132 West 31st Street
New York NY 10001

Library of Congress Cataloging-in-Publication Data

Lenburg, Jeff.
  Tex Avery : Hollywood's master of screwball cartoons / Jeff Lenburg. — 1st ed.
      p. cm. — (Legends of animation)
  Includes bibliographical references and index.
  ISBN-13: 978-1-60413-835-1 (hardcover : alk. paper)
  ISBN-10: 1-60413-835-1 (hardcover : alk. paper) 1. Avery, Tex, 1908—Juvenile literature. 2. Animators—United States—Biography—Juvenile literature. I. Avery, Tex, 1908- II. Title. III. Series.

  NC1766.U52A92355 2011
  791.4302'33092--dc22
  [B]
                        2010043706

Chelsea House books are available at special discounts when purchased in bulk quantities for businesses, associations, institutions, or sales promotions. Please call our Special Sales Department in New York at (212) 967-8800 or (800) 322-8755.

You can find Chelsea House on the World Wide Web at
http://www.chelseahouse.com

Text design by Kerry Casey
Cover design by Takeshi Takahashi
Composition by Kerry Casey
Cover printed by Yurchak Printing, Landisville, Pa.
Book printed and bound by Yurchak Printing, Landisville, Pa.
Date printed: April 2011

Printed in the United States of America

10 9 8 7 6 5 4 3 2 1

This book is printed on acid-free paper.

All links and Web addresses were checked and verified to be correct at the time of publication. Because of the dynamic nature of the Web, some addresses and links may have changed since publication and may no longer be valid.

To the original mad scientist and master of mayhem
(and exploding door stops) growing up,
my brother John, with love.

CONTENTS

ACKNOWLEDGMENTS

Special thanks to many individuals and organizations for their contributions of their time, talent, and material over the years for the completion of this project.

First and foremost my thanks to three legends of animation—the late Bob Clampett, Friz Freleng, and Walter Lantz—for sharing their memories of their dear colleague and friend, Tex Avery, in interviews I originally conducted for the formative chapter on Avery's career in my book, *The Great Cartoon Directors*.

Furthermore, I wish to thank Joe Adamson, Mark Kausler, Greg Lenburg, Bob Nelson, Steve Schneider, Randy Skretvedt; the Academy of Motion Picture Arts and Sciences Margaret Herrick Library, Metro-Goldwyn-Mayer, the Museum of Modern Art, Walter Lantz Productions, and Warner Bros. Inc.; and Eddie Brandt's Saturday Matinee, Larry Edmunds Bookshop, and MovieGoods.

Most of all, my sincere thanks to the late Tex Avery for the many years of laughter he provided. Without his comic genius and contributions to the field of animation, this book would not have been possible.

The Birth of a Cartoon Revolutionary

This self-styled anarchist made "What's up, Doc?" a standard salutation of the mainstream and created for audiences some of the world's most memorable characters ever to cavort across the silver screen: Bugs Bunny, Daffy Duck, Egghead, Droopy, George and Junior, and Screwy Squirrel. He was also instrumental in the development of Porky Pig and Elmer Fudd (in part, a modified version of his character Egghead) into cartoon superstars.

In the '30s, '40s, and '50s, he broke the mold of cartoon comedy, stretching the boundaries of the medium to achieve things few ever imagined were possible in an animated film while influencing generations of animators and live-action comedy directors. His lightning-fast-paced, brash and abrasive, over-the-top style of animation, layered with silly puns, visual gags, and throwaway bits, defy all logic in extraordinary ways. In his cartoons, characters go beyond the usual comic pratfall. They are splattered and squished like they are contortionists, or they literally fall apart, registering their surprise reactions on screen by doing extreme double takes. Their eyes pop out of their sockets. Their jaws spring to the floor. Their tongues rattle as they give a frightening high-pitched scream.

Often the joke is on the audience. After a sleek limousine motors across the screen, taking literally seconds for it pass through the frame, a sign on the rear bumper reads: "Long, Isn't It." Or the camera slowly pans across an open, grassy field where a herd of sheep innocently grazes, and stops at a sign hanging from a barbed wire fence that reads: "Cattle Country. Keep Out. This Means Ewe."

Little was sacred or out of bounds. As one writer noted of this cartoon legend, "…no bit of folklore was safe in his grasp." He made a sex object out of Little Red Riding Hood, mocked travelogues and documentaries, parodied famous Hollywood celebrities, classic fairytales, Westerns, and history, and created comical romps about modern society and modern inventions rendering audiences delirious with laughter. This is pretty remarkable for a man who never desired to be an animator in the first place.

He will be forever remembered as Hollywood's cartoon screwball master. He is Tex Avery.

Tex embarked on a propitious career in animation purely by fate. A lineal descendant of both the hanging judge Roy Bean and legendary frontiersman Daniel Boone, Frederick Bean Avery was born on February 26, 1908, as the elder son to Mary A. "Jessie" Bean and George W. Avery, a house designer and builder, in the small town of Taylor, Texas, located smack dab in the middle of the state in Williamson County. His father and mother were Southerners at heart. His dad was born in Alabama and his mother in Mississippi.

Tex grew up accustomed to a slow-paced, rural way of life. Despite its size, Taylor, founded in 1876 and originally named Taylorsville after International and Great Northern Railroad executive Edward Moses Taylor, was Tex's kind of place and kind of people. The town was known for its ethnic and civic pride and diverse population of red-blooded, hardworking, God-fearing Texans—neighborly citizens who practiced good, old-fashioned values, who cared about their community and fellow neighbors, and who helped others without expecting anything in return but a hearty handshake or a simple "thank you." As a major agricultural hub where cotton farming was a mainstay, Taylor became a

Tex Avery is best known by some of the cartoon characters he created, such as Droopy, a dog, seen here in this theatrical poster for Droopy's debut, *Dumb-Hounded*, in 1943. © *Metro-Goldwyn-Mayer*.

leading producer in the state, due to the area's rich, abundant soil and temperate climate. Migrant workers came to Taylor from far and wide to harvest crops and perform the grueling, backbreaking work of picking cotton by hand. Taylor was also known for its clean streets and serene neighborhoods and two-story, stately mansions, built before the turn of the century, and its major cultural event of the year—its annual fair.

It was in this simple, yet robust place that, at age 13, Tex discovered his true love: cartooning. He committed himself to becoming a cartoonist and dabbled in drawing right up until he attended North Dallas High School. Built in 1922, the three-story brick-and-mortar school building, now part of the Dallas Independent School District and located in the Oak Lawn suburb, is the oldest high school in the Dallas area. In showcasing his talent, Avery annually filled the pages of *The Viking* yearbook with humorously and awkwardly drawn cartoons of school activities, because he was, as he once said, "the only guy who could handle a pencil." Besides illustrating the school's yearbook and monthly magazine, he also freelance drew a weekly one-panel cartoon strip that he posted on the school's bulletin boards and which drew large crowds of curious onlookers that often "jammed traffic in the halls."

Tex was like many other kids born and bred in the area. A loner and perfectionist from an early age, he enjoyed many other passions besides cartooning. One of them was athletics. He likewise enjoyed recreational activities—fishing and shooting. His favorite shooting sport was duck hunting, which he started doing at Dallas's White Rock Lake. He later claimed the lake as "Daffy Duck's birthplace."

At age 18, Tex graduated from high school and immediately tried landing work in his field. He hounded the offices of local newspaper cartoonists. Many of those that reviewed his drawings suggested his work would be much improved if he obtained proper art training.

Without hesitation, Tex enrolled in a three-month summer course at the Art Institute of Chicago, originally founded as the Chicago Academy of Fine Arts in 1879 and renamed three years later. Functioning as both trade school and museum of modern art, the facility was located downtown on a park-like setting at Michigan Avenue and Adams Street. He took courses at night and learned the ins and outs of life drawing, still drawing, color, and composition. Tex also learned from industry professionals who would talk shop in his classes, including such notables as Pulitzer-winning *Chicago Tribune* cartoonist John T. McCutcheon.

For someone as free-spirited and strong-willed as Tex, the Art Institute did not turn out to be a good fit. After just one month, he quit. He found the whole experience distasteful. As he once recalled, "They gave me all kinds of life study but what good is that to a cartoonist? It made me tired, so I quit."

Tex remained in the famed Windy City for a short time thereafter, exploring other opportunities. He met with many well-known comic strip artists in the city, for their advice about jobs in the profession. But after receiving little encouragement from them, he packed his bags and went back home, where he contemplated his future. One thing about Tex that rang true throughout his life: People often underestimated him. The young Texan had a fiery desire to succeed. Not even this latest setback would hold him back. When he made up his mind, nothing could stop him.

HEADING TO HOLLYWOOD

Tex decided he would go west. On New Year's Day, 1928, he enthusiastically drove with a few friends from Dallas to Los Angeles in search of work as a comic strip artist. Planning only to stay six weeks, he was so instantly snake-bitten by the lure of Hollywood and its sunny, arid climate that he chose to stay.

Making his home in Los Angeles, Tex peddled his cartoon strips by day in hopes of finding a buyer; by night, he worked the late evening to early morning shift, loading fruit and vegetable crates on the docks, and slept on the beaches. Remembering those days, he said, "You would be surprised how warm and soft a beach is after working all night. And that's when I'd get a lot of practice drawing. I'd sketch everything that came my way (if I wasn't asleep)."

Tex kept working on his cartoon strip and after improving his rough artwork and storylines, he submitted samples "everywhere" to magazine and newspaper editors. For his efforts, he received a pile of rejections and found breaking into the business with his own strip fruit-less. One business that was thriving in Hollywood, however, was car-toon animation. One day, a kid who happened to spy on his so-called cartoon "scratchings" at the beach encouraged him to apply at the local Charles Mintz animation studio. Tex had never considered working in animation, saying "animation to me was nothing." He wasted no time, however, and immediately camped out at the studio until he was hired a few months later as a cel inker and painter.

In 1930, Tex jumped ship to work in a similar position at the Walter Lantz Studio after a guy who lived across the street from him—whose girlfriend was the head of the studio's inking and painting depart-ment—urged him to apply. The studio, originally located in a barnlike structure, was producing 26 *Oswald the Lucky Rabbit* cartoon shorts for Universal Films and was seeking young artists to bolster its depleted corps. Many animators who signed on with the studio migrated west from the New York animation industry. Lantz inherited the *Oswald* series two years after Walt Disney, who originally produced it through an arrangement with his distributor Charles Mintz, had lost the rights to the character.

Tex gave the position his all and understood how fortunate he was to be hired since he was not a great animator, just a good one. As he told author Joe Adamson: "I never was too great an artist. I realized there at Lantz's that most of these fellows could draw rings around me. I could put it over crudely, and that was enough to get by at the time, but a lot of these guys, your top Disney men, as far as anatomy or what-not—hell, you can't touch 'em!"

For the longest time, Tex pursued his heartfelt desire to become a newspaper cartoonist while maintaining that he had "no interest in animation" or in becoming an animator. As he admitted, "I kept send-ing in drawings and drawings but none were ever accepted." He viewed animation as something he would try, a momentary stopover until he sold his strip and his dream of becoming a successful comic strip artist was realized. But the onslaught of rejections told him otherwise. Find-ing animation less frustrating, Avery permanently shelved his strip and any notion of making a living as a newspaper cartoonist. He realized that "animation was the coming thing" and thus channeled heart and soul toward a career in that field.

At the Lantz studio, Tex slowly worked his way up while inking and painting backgrounds on *Oswald* cartoons through the early 1930s, at which time he was promoted to in-betweener. In this role, he served as fill-in artist, sketching essential drawings that were important to the smooth, continuous movement of each character. As Tex once recalled, "I became an in-betweener and slowly learned the art of animation. Then, I drew a couple of storyboards and they worked out pretty well."

Shortly after his arrival, Tex also worked as a gagman, frequently pitching original gags that made their way to the screen in several *Oswald* cartoons. His slapstick style was largely influenced by Charlie Chaplin and Mack Sennett comedies from the silent era, which featured contrived and impossible gags carried out in live-action that produced huge laughs in movie theaters. The heavy influence of Tex's outrageous sense of humor permeated such films as *The Singing Sap, Hell's Heels*, and *The Prison Panic*, released to movie theaters in 1930.

In a short period of time, Tex was elevated to assistant animator. His duties were to draw sequential sketches for main or extreme character poses in the *Oswald* cartoons. Then, after Walt Disney raided West Coast studios for talent to add to his animation studio, three-quarters of the staffers that remained "knew nothing of animation," only in-betweening.

BEGINNING THE MADNESS AND THE MAYHEM

The depletion of staff turned out to be fortuitous for Tex. Bill Nolan, a pioneer animator who had directed several successful cartoon series in New York since the early days of animation, had joined the Lantz studio as a director, after writing, producing, and directing his first independent series, *Newslaffs*. Under his agreement with Lantz, Nolan was responsible for producing half of the studio's annual output of 26 cartoons. He and Lantz each had their own animation units and directed or codirected films together. After eyeing the noticeable upswing of Avery's humor in the *Oswald* films, Nolan named Tex and Ray Abrams as head

Avery developed his trademark brand of screwball comedy early in his career and later used it for cartoons such as his hilarious take on ventriloquism gone wild, *Ventriloquist Cat* (1950). © *Metro-Goldwyn-Mayer.*

animators on the series. The result was more Avery-flavored films that Nolan directed. This included breaking down that invisible barrier—or fourth wall—between characters and his audience that started with Tex's work at the Lantz studio.

One such cartoon was *In The Zoo*, released in 1933. The film was typical of Tex's unrestrained humor and why it struck a chord with Nolan and moviegoers. In one scene, the character, Pegleg Pete, opens a can of moths on a bear that proceed to eat the bear's fur coat, leaving him with only his underwear to cover him. Reacting unlike anything audiences would expect, the bear calmly studies himself and then deadpans to the audience, "Well, imagine that!" Such classic cartoon mayhem would be common in Tex's work throughout his career.

For the finished scene, Tex's comical device was to "have the bear stripped naked." But when he was unable to decide how to exit the scene—either have the bear do an outrageous double take, blush, or exit screaming—he thought of his audience and asked his fellow animators in his unit, "What do you think the audience would least expect this bear to do?" He ultimately answered his own question: "How would it be if they chew the fur off this bear, and then he looks right up to the audience and says, 'Well, whaddya know about that?'" That, in a nutshell, was the premise behind Avery's stock-and-trade humor: Do the opposite of what audiences expected and leave them laughing in the process.

Besides writing and selling gags to Nolan that were used in the *Oswald* cartoons, Avery also wrote two stories after Nolan suggested, "Why don't you do a story?" Working under Nolan, however, was often a challenge. By this point in Nolan's career, he had become increasingly disenchanted with the whole animation industry. Prone to acts of laziness, he regularly pawned off more of his responsibility to Tex to finish half of his animation output—accounting for three to four minutes of animation in a single cartoon—and to "gag it up." As animator Leo Salkin later recalled, "Where Lantz was desirous of doing a funny film, Bill just wanted to make it through these things."

Although Tex appeared to find his niche, he still was not content with his progress. He had no ill feelings about his job or boss. Instead, he was upset at himself for not producing "good enough drawings."

Many years later, after someone screened for him the first scene he ever animated in a Lantz cartoon, Tex was boorish about his talent. "As soon as the scene came on, I remembered it! Gee whiz, what a lousy scene! Just a big bunch of nothing!" he said.

The perfectionist that he was, Tex was concerned that he could not finish a cleaned drawing; he always had to have another animator smooth out the rough edges for him. In order to rectify the situation, he spent long hours at the studio and stayed up late at home to work on his drawings. In the end, he triumphed and had the last laugh. While other animators were more talented and could outdraw him and their technique was more refined, it was his outrageous invention and perfect execution of wild visual gags and slapstick humor that set him apart.

The husky and robust Texan became a popular fixture at the Lantz studio, embraced by his colleagues. It was not uncommon for other gag-men and animators to hang around his desk and swap ideas and gags, and stories that eventually wound up on the screen in some fashion.

In addition to his fertile comic mind, Tex possessed another important asset that made him likeable to his peers: humility. As former Warner Brothers' story man Michael Maltese once said: "He'd rather back off then step forward and take justifiable bows." That was normal for Tex, remembers author Joe Adamson, who has said that he never acknowledged himself in times of glory and credit. He always used "we" during the course of his conversation, passing credit onto others.

Lantz didn't have a story department in those days, so he would meet with the animators and assistants in the evening every two weeks to hash out ideas. Calling Tex "a rapid practical joker," he was immediately impressed by the young animator's "natural talent, especially his exaggerated sense of humor...Everyone contributed gags, but Tex was the outstanding contributor and the funniest," Lantz said.

Coming up with gags for each film, in Tex's opinion, was a collaborative effort. After returning to Dallas in the spring of 1933, his first time back in his native state since moving to Los Angeles, the 25-year-old animator happily discussed, in an interview with the *Dallas Morning News*, the working methods and processes of developing gags for cartoons at the Lantz studio. During their meetings with Lantz, he and other animators and gagmen would have more gags than they could actually use because they were, as he described, "a pretty hard bunch to please." Consequently, not every gag that was suggested made it into the final cartoon.

In his case, Tex had a real knack for finding humor in not-so-obvious places. One gag he developed was for a Western cartoon—a shoot-out between the hero and the villain when they fire their six-shooters at each other. As he described, "There was a cut and the next scene showed a little bullet and a very large one running towards each other in mid-air. The little bullet saw the big one, squealed weakly and ran back into the barrel of the hero's gun."

For Tex, comedy had no limits. In those days, studios routinely placed limits on how much footage animators could animate for each cartoon. That was not the case at the Lantz studio, where he was once assigned to animate a short ship scene in an *Oswald the Lucky Rabbit* cartoon, *Chris Columbus Jr.* (1934), of Oswald's nemesis, the peg-legged pirate Louie the Lug, lighting and firing a cannon. Tex turned the fairly simple assignment into a huge comedy routine by the time he was finished. He gagged up the scene with the cannon drooping and the cannon ball rolling out, and then pointing the cannon straight up so when Louie would try to light the fuse, it would suddenly go out. Subsequently, he expanded the scene from 10 feet to 60 feet of footage, and after Lantz saw it, he said, "Heck, yeah, we'll leave it in."

Tex's non sequitur left animators laughing and had the same effect on theater audiences. In the world of cartoon comedy, he was quickly leaving his indelible mark.

2

Unleashing the Lunacy at Warner Bros.

With his failure to become a newspaper cartoonist a distant memory, Tex appeared happy with his life. The energetic animator, with his stylish, pencil-thin mustache, full coif of dark hair, and wide contagious grin, was making a good living, earning around $75 a week, and loving his Southern California lifestyle.

What Tex never expected was suddenly being thrust into the role of director. In 1935, the moody Nolan left the Lantz studio. Prior to his departure, in one of his typical displays of laziness, he dumped two *Oswald* cartoons on Tex to direct, preceded by the edict, "Do them."

Seizing the opportunity, Tex accepted the jobs of directing with typical aplomb and humility. It is believed he directed without receiving screen credit—with directing credit given to Lantz instead—*The Hillbilly* (the last *Oswald* that Nolan co-directed before his departure), *Towne Hall Follies*, and *The Quail Hunt*, all released in 1935.

Tex enjoyed the experience so much that he realized he was better suited as a director than an animator since most of his fellow animators at Lantz, as he once said, "could draw rings" around him. He decided at that moment, "Why fight it. I'll never make it! Go the other route!"

Personally speaking, Tex's life profoundly changed during this time. After a series of relationships that went nowhere, he met and married the one woman who stole his heart: Patricia Johnson. A former film actress and extra, she sought a different line of work after growing weary of "being chased around desks by casting agents," and landed a job in the ink and paint department at the Lantz studio, where they met.

Also during this time, the normally jocular animator suffered a tragedy that altered his life forever. One day at the studio, during some office horseplay, a rowdy bunch of gagmen—who, in Tex's words, did "anything for a laugh"—were shooting paper spitballs with rubber bands at each other. One of them, Charles Hastings, went too far by using a steel paper clip in place of a spitball and slung it at him. After one of the guys close by yelled, "Look out, Tex!" Tex turned and the paper clip stabbed him directly in his left eye. He was left permanently handicapped, blind in that one eye, which was replaced by a fake eye.

Always self-conscious of his hefty size, Tex would routinely exercise, jog, or play volleyball at the Santa Monica beach, but after the eye incident, he was never the same. His self-esteem plummeted and his weight soared. Layout artist Bob Givens, who later worked with Avery at Warner Bros., said he was "kind of paranoid about it. Always kind of turned away from you. [Though] nobody could tell which was the fake." Years later, as a result of his lost sight, Tex consequently suggested that "the animation business owed me a living."

AIMING HIGHER: DIRECTING

In mid-1935, Tex called it quits at the Lantz studio when Universal Pictures, Lantz's cartoon distributor, refused to pay him the additional $10 to $15 a week he wanted. Rather than wallow in self-pity and defeatism, Tex used the circumstances surrounding his departure to embark on his true calling: directing.

By now, the field of animation had grown exponentially. With a number of studios in operation, including Walt Disney, Columbia Pictures, Fleischer, Metro-Goldwyn-Mayer, and Warner Bros., opportunities were plentiful elsewhere. Fortunately, Tex never had to sell himself to several studios at once. He landed a new job right away at a studio that was perfectly suited for his uninhibited high-octane humor and where he would leave a lasting mark.

Tex heard that Leon Schlesinger Productions, producers of Warner Bros. *Looney Tunes* and *Merrie Melodies* cartoons, was looking for another director to form a third unit. The 27-year-old animator eagerly met with the moon-faced producer Leon Schlesinger to interview for the position. During their meeting, he faked his way into the job, playing up his experience as a director of two cartoons at the Lantz studio, even though he never received screen credit for his work. Schlesinger, displeased with the work of his supervisor Tom Palmer, told Tex, "I'll try you. I'll try on you on one picture," and hired him on the spot. Later Tex admitted he was surprised Schlesinger jumped at the chance to hire him. "I don't know why or how Schlesinger gambled on me. Evidently he was quite desperate," he said.

Schlesinger's hiring of Tex gave the Schlesinger studio three full-time directors, with Tex joining fellow directors Isadore "Friz" Freleng and Jack King. Several terrific ex-Nolan animators from the Lantz studio followed him, including Virgil Ross, Sid Sutherland, Joe D'Igalo, and Jack Carr. Ross and Sutherland joined his unit along with three so-called "renegades," as Schlesinger called them, who were "unhappy" with the people they were working with: the young, eager-beaver animators Charles M. "Chuck" Jones, Bob Clampett, and Bob "Bobe" Cannon. Jones and Clampett, who years later became shining stars of the Warner Bros. cartoon division, provided Tex with one of the studio's most creative tandems, and Cannon, a terrific draftsman, went on to become an accomplished cartoon director at United Productions of America (UPA). Little did Schlesinger realize at the time of hiring Tex what a find he had in him: an animator whose innovative comedy approach and structure and slapstick gaggery would inspire and influence his Warner Bros. colleagues, including Freleng, Jones, Clampett, and Frank Tashlin, and who would become a major contributor in the development of the studio's most famous cartoon characters and distinctive style and brand of humor.

Tex Avery at the Warner Bros. lot. Avery *(second from left)* sits with *(from left to right)*: Frank Tashlin, Hendry Binder, producer Leon Schlesinger, Ray Katz, and Friz Freleng, circa 1936.

Right from the start, Tex transformed the studio's cartoons and the field of cartoon shorts with his rapid-fire, obsessively inventive directing style. Clampett, who joined Warner Bros. in early 1931 and worked on the very first Warner Bros. *Merrie Melodies* cartoon, noted that by 1935, before his arrival, "a certain staleness and predictability in the use and reuse of the same general story formats and gags had set in. It was as if a hard crust had formed over the creative process, and those of us that suggested newer wackier ideas felt as if we were hitting our head against a stone wall. It was at this propitious moment that Tex Avery came on the scene."

Clampett credits Tex for breaking through "the hard crust" and for eventually changing the style and content of Warner Bros. cartoons as well as influencing the entire cartoon industry. "To those of us who poured through the breach with him," he once said, "it will remain one of the most exhilarating and cherished memories of our lifetime."

As critic Leonard Maltin writes in his cartoon studio history, *Of Mice and Magic*, "Tex Avery, perhaps more than any other single person in animation, perfected the art of the gag cartoon…Avery knew how to make the most of the cartoon medium. He had no interest in duplicating or imitating reality. In his mind the broader and the more unreal, the better."

Cramped for space due to the sudden expansion of staff, Schlesinger temporarily relegated Tex and his unit to a small, white, wood-framed, five-room one-story bungalow in the middle of the Warner Bros. Sunset Boulevard lot completely isolated from the Schlesinger studio. The ramshackle building, infested with termites, was quickly dubbed "Termite Terrace," a nickname later used to describe the entire Schlesinger/Warner Bros. cartoon studio. Schlesinger also put Tex's unit there to avoid "tipping off" Palmer that he was about to be fired. Tex's unit was assigned mostly to working on the studio's black-and-white *Looney Tunes* cartoon series.

Tex later reflected approvingly of Schlesinger's decision to move them into that "little shack." "He was smart; he didn't disturb us," he said. "We were all alone out there, and he knew nothing that went on."

BREAKING CONVENTIONS WITH A PIG NAMED PORKY

Tex and his animation unit exceeded Schlesinger's expectations admirably. For his first directing assignment, Tex reviewed the studio's previous releases, searching for potential starring characters and settled on Porky and Beans from Friz Freleng's *I Haven't Got a Hat*, a spoof of Hal Roach's popular live-action *Our Gang* short-subject series, which featured the plump stuttering pig (Porky) trying to recite a poem. After seeing the character, Tex enthused, "Let's try a pig," and sold Schlesinger on the idea. He built a story around both characters, changing them into adults.

Building on his desire to impress Schlesinger and break from the studio's past by doing something more wildly imaginative and entertaining, Tex ushered in a new era at Warner Bros. with the release of his first *Looney Tunes* cartoons animated by Clampett and Jones, *Gold Diggers of '49*, starring Porky Pig, Beans, and Little Kitty. While directing the second cartoon in the studio's history featuring Porky, Tex largely changed the characters to his liking. Porky is drawn more like a big hog and Beans is more refined, unlike the saucy young cat paired with Porky in Freleng's effort, *I Haven't Got a Hat*. The storyline is classic Avery: a comical melodrama set in the gold rush of the 1840s, with Beans having to retrieve a valuable sack stolen from Porky in exchange for his hand in marriage to Porky's daughter (played by Little Kitty), who is also kidnapped. The movie provides a glimpse of the ingredients that set Tex's work apart from his counterparts: using hyperbole and exaggeration for comical effect. For example, in one scene, Porky announces to a man taking a bath in a tub outdoors that he has discovered gold. Embarrassed, the man picks up his tub and quickly runs off screen with the tub wrapped around his waist like a barrel for laughs.

Impressed by the film's faster pace and imaginative flair, which made it markedly funnier than those of Schlesinger's other two directors, Schlesinger kept Tex on. Tex's subsequent Warner Bros. cartoons would further establish his distinctive style and joyous blend of exaggerated timing, frenetic madcap humor, and the absurd that would become his hallmark. As a result, Schlesinger assigned Tex to direct additional Porky Pig cartoon shorts, helping turn the stammering pig into the studio's first legitimate star.

Tex and his staff seized their opportunity with reckless abandon, transferring that creative madness onto the screen. Determined to create wilder and funnier gags in every cartoon, Tex created a working environment that was "gaggy" and "fun," drawing the best out of his staff. "We worked every night—Jones, Clampett, and I were all young and full of ambition," he later said. "My gosh, nothing stopped us!"

The atmosphere at Warner Bros. was "real loose" and the animators all had fun. "There's never been a studio like that," recalled Maltese, adding, "Usually anybody working for a director would say, 'He's the boss,' and there would be problems. But Avery would cheer the guys into this crazy mixed-up attitude."

Clampett found Tex likeable and a great story man, gagman, and innovator. As he recalled, "I was supposed to help Tex with his stories. He'd almost always originate the angle himself, and then he and I would work together gaggling the stories Tex directed. I would sometimes help him with layouts, and then animate. Tex's first cartoons were all funny, and all good."

Warner Bros. legend Chuck Jones, later memorializing Tex, said, "I learned from him the most important truth about animation: Animation is the art of timing, a truth applicable as well to all motion pictures. And the most brilliant masters of timing were usually comedians: Keaton, Chaplin, Laurel and Hardy, Langdon—and Fred (Tex) Avery."

Until then, Jones had never experienced anyone quite like Tex. He "was lightning. Just as unpredictable, as surprising, as spectacular as lightning—with one difference: Unlike lightning, Avery was funny." As Jones added, "He did the most incredible things. He was extending the graphics of animation."

In working alongside Tex, Jones admitted, "I was ignorant of his genius as I suppose Michaelangelo's apprentices were oblivious to the fact they too were working with genius. In spite of that intellectual weakness on my part, Avery's brilliance penetrated the husk of my self-assured ignorance, the ignorance that encases most 20-year-olds."

Tex was "not one to pontificate," Jones said, "but for all of us who worked with him and beside him the message was loud and clear; by his example he taught us."

In 1936, Tex helmed nine more cartoons, demonstrating for movie audiences his spontaneous zest for the zaniest. First up was his second *Looney Tunes* cartoon, *Plane Dippy,* released that January, the first starring Porky Pig and first animated by Virgil Ross, in which Porky joins the U.S. Army Air Corps to learn to fly, but is victimized by an out-of-control robot plane. That April, Tex directed his third *Looney Tunes* cartoon and his second starring Porky Pig, *The Blow Out.* This time Porky tangles with a mad bomber who is terrorizing the city.

Up until then, Tex had directed strictly *Looney Tunes*, but that year he would also supervise his first of four *Merrie Melodies* cartoons. As he did with Porky Pig, he put his own personal stamp on his *Merrie Melodies* shorts, structuring them around an ensemble of spot gags and swing music. The first of these, distributed that March, was the experimental short, *Miss Glory*, employing rich and distinctive-looking Art Deco backgrounds and character designs and a Busby Berkeley-musical theme in which a small-town bellhop's dream of working in a chic New York hotel turns into a nightmare. As often was the case in Warner Bros. cartoons, the animators also referenced themselves in the film by featuring caricatures of Bob Clampett, Chuck Jones, Bob Cannon, Melvin Millar, and Tex himself.

Tex's ensuing *Merrie Melodies* releases that year once again displayed his comical handiwork and knack for the absurd: *I'd Love to Take Orders from You*, a comical take on Father Scarecrow teaching his son, Junior, the ins and outs of "scarecrowing;" *I Love to Singa* (1936), Avery's spoof of Al Jolson's *The Jazz Singer* (1927), starring a cursed piano-teaching owl in the Jolson role as "Owl Jolson"; and *Don't Look Now*, a St. Valentine's Day love affair involving Cupid and a lonely skunk, issued to theaters that December.

Meanwhile, Tex exerted tremendous influence over the development of his first starring character, Porky Pig, directing three new original *Looney Tunes* that season, two of them shaped around the precept of Porky as a hero. In *Porky the Rain-Maker*, distributed to theaters that August, Porky and his Poppa's farm is endangered by drought until Porky buys a bottle of Rain Pills at a medicine show that causes abundant rain fall on their thirsty crops. Tex repeats this formula in *Milk and Money*, issued that October, in which Porky saves his Poppa from losing his farm to a slimy landlord, Mr. Viper, after Porky accidentally enters a horse race and wins the grand prize of $10,000.

Porky goes from hero to goat in Tex's third effort, *The Village Smithy*. Released in 1936, it was a warped version of the classic poem, "The Village Blacksmith," by Henry Wadsworth Longfellow. Porky, playing a blacksmith's assistant, gives a horse a "hot foot" with a hot horseshoe and the horse runs off with the blacksmith in tow. Tex uses an off-screen narrator in this cartoon, claiming to be the first to use such a device in a cartoon and that it was "the only thing Disney ever stole from us."

While the Warner Bros. cartoons Tex masterminded during this period were generally held in high regard by critics, his famously fastidious and persistently prankish style of comedy was about to foster an even higher caliber of achievements to come.

3

Plain Daffy

Every artist or performer experiences a major turning point in their career. For Tex, his came in threes. A pivotal year for him at Warner Bros., 1937 was when he became firmly established as top Hollywood auteur in the animation industry.

Tex further developed Porky Pig, which he redesigned, into a major star. Porky became a top box-office draw under his direction, as was the case in several new cartoon shorts released that year exhibiting his patented ingredients for humor. One was *Porky the Wrestler* (1937). Released that January, Porky is mistaken for a boxing challenger when he enters the ring during a wrestling match. The cartoon was the first film animated by new member of Tex's unit, Elmer Wait, who died some months after the cartoon was released.

Another superb Porky Pig effort by Tex, distributed to theaters a month later, was *Picador Porky* (1937). Porky enters to win 1,000 pesos in a Mexican bullfighting contest and expects to fight a phony bull (his friends in costume) but instead comes face-to-face with a real bull! The cartoon had special significance as it was the first cartoon to feature the voice of Mel Blanc, who made his mark on radio before joining Warner Bros., where he would supply his voice for practically every major studio character and then some.

Blanc landed his first voice gig at Warner Bros. thanks in part to Tex. In December 1936, after making numerous rounds to Leon Schlesinger Productions seeking to audition for the casting director only to be turned away, Blanc finally won entry into the studio after he encountered a different person at the front desk who knew nothing of his past attempts and was seated there because the guy who usually worked the desk had died a week earlier.

A lively Christmas party was under way in the cartoon division when Blanc entered with all four of the studio's directors on hand—Tex, Friz Freleng, Frank Tashlin, and Bob Clampett. Impressed by Blanc's routine, Tex said to him, "Hey, Mel, I've got this new cartoon character in the works, and you might be the person for his voice."

Blanc said, "What kind of character is it?"

Running into his office, Tex returned producing a drawing of a bull. "We need a drunken bull. Think you can do it?"

Blanc, who had played a drunk on radio's Judy Canova show as a regular, gave Tex exactly what he was looking for. He transformed himself into the drunken bull by scrunching up his face, squinting through one eye, and affecting a lazy Southern drawl punctuated by hiccups. Tex loved the bit and put Blanc to work, scheduling him for a recording session to do that same voice in the film.

A DARN FOOL DUCK AND A REAL EGGHEAD

Two other important milestones followed that year when Tex created and introduced two new characters to movie audiences. The first was a loony little black duck he cast opposite Porky. As author Steve Schneider writes, he did "crazy things for no apparent purpose, delighting in his dementia and maintaining a pace no live-action counterpart could ever compete with." This vintage black-and-white *Looney Tunes* production, *Porky's Duck Hunt*, released that April was Tex's wackiest Warner Bros. cartoon to date and introduced none other than Daffy Duck. Animated by Bob Clampett, Daffy is far more deranged in his film debut and used more like a bit player returning periodically throughout the story, in which the shotgun-toting duck hunter, Porky, is out to snatch a duck (Daffy) for dinner.

The Crazy-
Darnfool
Duck

COMPARATIVE SIZES
OF
CHARACTERS

Animator Bob Clampett drew this comparative model sheet of Tex
Avery's "crazy darn fool duck," Daffy Duck, and Porky Pig for Daffy's
first film appearance, *Porky's Duck Hunt* (1937). *Courtesy Bob Clampett
Collection.*

Daffy serves as the comic relief, foiling Porky's and his loyal hound's
efforts to bag him for supper. He giddily laughs at his own jokes, spoil-
ing Porky's fun and telling him, "Don't let it worry you, skipper—I'm
just a crazy darnfool duck!" as he manically handsprings and dances
across the lake crying, "Who-hoo! Who-hoo!" In later films helmed by
Warner Bros. directors Bob Clampett, Friz Freleng, and Chuck Jones,
Daffy was transformed from a deranged whirligig to more of an oddball

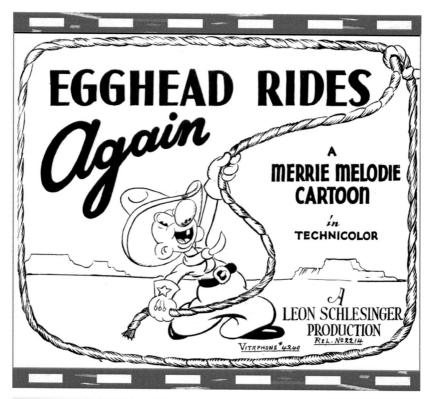

Avery's favorite cartoon sap, Egghead, is pictured on the lobby card from the *Merrie Melodies* cartoon *Egghead Rides Again* (1937). © *Warner Bros.*

and comic foil whose devilish schemes often backfired. Nonetheless, soon he would exceed Porky in popularity as his star status reached a fever pitch with audiences. As Clampett said of Daffy's debut, "At that time, audiences weren't accustomed to seeing a cartoon character do these things. And so, when it hit the theaters it was like an explosion. People would leave the theaters talking about this daffy duck."

Following Daffy's onscreen arrival that year was Tex's second creation: a rail-thin, bulbous-nosed buffoon named Egghead, first unveiled in *Egghead Rides Again*. This cartoon sap, topped off by a derby hat, high-collar shirt, and ill-fitting suit, was based on a famous nightclub comedian, Ben Blue, and voiced by actor Cliff Nazarro, whose vocal characterization imitated a popular radio comedian of that era, Joe Penner of "Wanna buy a duck?" fame. Penner was under contract with Warner Bros. in 1937 to star in two-reel comedy shorts and features. Egghead later morphed into that dim-wit hunter Elmer Fudd and appeared in more than a dozen cartoons, nine directed by Tex, in various roles either as a star or walk-on character.

Egghead made his second film appearance that November in Tex's first fairy-tale spoof, *Little Red Walking Hood*, based on the classic children's fairy tale, *Little Red Riding Hood* and complete with his version of Red, whose voice and manner is reminiscent of actress Katharine Hepburn, and the Wolf (voiced by story man Tedd Pierce). With backgrounds designed and drawn entirely in color pencils by Tex's favorite background artist, Johnny Johnsen (also credited at times as John Didrik Johnsen), and animation by Irv Spence (later a principal animator of Hanna-Barbera's MGM *Tom and Jerry* cartoons), the storybook-styled, one-reel short established the overall tone, pace, and comic formula Tex used in other fairy-tale satires to come under the Warner Bros. banner, including *Cinderella Meets Fella* (1938), starring Egghead, and *The Bear's Tale* (1940), featuring Goldilocks and the Three Bears.

In *Little Red Walking Hood*, Egghead periodically pops up throughout the film at the most unexpected places, whistling a tune and carrying a violin case until his appearance is finally questioned, "Who the heck are you anyway?"

Egghead comically replies, "I'm the hero in this picture." Then, suddenly producing a mallet from his violin case, he clobbers the Wolf with it.

Tex continued perfecting his visual and verbal comic assault on audiences, characteristically using Egghead as his hero of the moment in upcoming films. One such film was the *Merrie Melodies* cartoon *The Isle of Pingo Pongo* (1937), Tex's first in a series of spot-gag and mock-travelogue cartoons cowritten by him and Bob Clampett (who is uncredited) and that employed an off-screen narrator to lampoon film producer, director, writer, and narrator James A. Fitzpatrick's live-action travelogue series, *Traveltalks*, for MGM.

Tex initially developed a series of gags for the film but had nothing to tie them together. So he added a running gag of the simpleton Egghead as comic relief, carrying a violin and asking the pompous, off-camera narrator every time he segues into a new scene, "Now, Boss?" with the narrator politely retorting, "No, not now. Sorry!"

This gag recurs throughout the short, with Egghead repeating the same refrain but the narrator retorting more firmly each time, "No!" In spoofing the Fitzpatrick travelogues, Tex, in particular, pokes fun at the ending of those shorts in which the narrator gushes: "And now, we leave you as the sun sinks slowly in the west," but with a twist. As the narrator continues, "As the suns sinks slowly in the west," the sun never sinks.

Finally, Egghead comes to the rescue, his violin case in tow, and again asks, "Now, Boss?"

Frustrated, the narrator says, "Yes, now!"

Egghead brandishes a rifle out of his violin case. He shoots the sun, which immediately drops out of the scene, as the narrator adds in parting, "Goodnight!"

One unintended consequence of Tex's film was it being later banned from television syndication in 1968 as part of the library of Warner Bros. cartoons distributed to television by United Artists, deemed too racially offensive due to his portrayal of the black, island natives with excessively large lips and feet in the film.

As in his previous film appearances, Egghead either starred or sporadically interrupted the goings-on in later cartoon releases directed by Tex. In the *Merrie Melodies* release *Johnny Smith and Poker-Huntas* (1938), his comical rendition of the historic Mayflower landing, Egghead, as Johnny Smith (Avery's caricatured version of the real Mayflower Captain Johnny Smith), encounters a tribe of Indians who aren't friendly but utterly sarcastic! Later that year, Egghead would appear in another *Merrie Melodies* cartoon, *A Feud There Was* (1938), for the first time under the name of Elmer Fudd (named after Avery unit animator Elmer Wait) in Tex's satirical version of the famous Hatfield–McCoy feud involving two warring hillbilly families. The yodeling, bulbous-nosed Elmer plays peacemaker to bring the so-named Weaver and McCoy families together, only to end up on the wrong end of things as the furious families open fire on him after he makes a yodeling exit.

Egghead gets pummeled in a boxing match after taking a correspondence course in Avery's *Merrie Melodies* cartoon, *Count Me Out* (1938). *Courtesy MovieGoods. © Warner Bros.*

Under Tex's exceptional direction, Egghead stole the show again in three more releases. In *Believe It or Else* (1939), a laugh-out-loud parody of newsreels, Egghead walks on the screen in mock protest throughout the short carrying signs proclaiming, "I don't believe it" or "It's a Fake." In *Hamateur Night* (1939), Tex's spoof of vaudeville amateur nights released in late January, every bad act that performs is hissed, booed, and pelted by tomatoes on stage until Egghead sings his off-key rendition of "She'll Be Coming 'Round the Mountain" and unanimously wins the top prize, to wild applause of an audience made up entirely of Eggheads!

Finally, in *A Day at the Zoo* (1939), Tex makes the most of Egghead's last screen appearance in this farce of zoo documentaries building up to comical payoff at the end between a series of spot gags starring a hodge-podge cast of animals with nonsensical names—camels "smoking" cigarettes; an "Alcatraz jailbird" and "stool pigeon;" and a skunk engrossed in reading a book, *How to Win Friends and Influence People*—and a running gag of Egghead taunting a huge ferocious lion. The off-camera narrator warns the silly sap every time of the dangers, but Egghead persists until finally, at the end of the cartoon, the lion appears suddenly more content and wider in girth as he opens his mouth to reveal the whites of two eyes blinking in the pitch darkness of his stomach, with Egghead crying a comical tag line made famous by comedian Lou Costello, "I'm a baaad boy!"

Egghead would fully transition into the character Elmer Fudd in the 1940 Bugs Bunny cartoon *Elmer's Candid Camera*, directed by Avery protégé Chuck Jones.

Of all of Tex's cartoons featuring Egghead, perhaps the most significant was the full-color *Merrie Melodies* cartoon released to theaters on January 1, 1938, *Daffy Duck and Egghead*, the studio's first starring Daffy Duck and the first of many more to come that would establish Daffy as a rising star.

Upset by a shadowy figure in the audience who stands up in the beginning of the cartoon and will not sit down, Egghead, sporting a red plaid hunter's cap and beige hunting jacket and carrying a large shotgun, shoots the fool who proceeds to go through an extended death scene. Egghead then hunts Daffy after the maniacal mallard lures him into the tall grass and then jumps up and bites him on the nose. Daffy parlays his practical joke into a series of events that leave Egghead frustrated, like when Daffy makes Egghead shoot an apple on his head. When he misses, Daffy hands him a sign that reads "Blind," a cup of pencils, and then slaps a pair of dark glasses on his nose and comically retorts, "Too bad, too bad."

To his delight, the lisping Daffy breaks into song and sings his own version of the *Looney Tunes* theme, "The Merry-Go-Round Broke Down," at the same time establishing his personality for movie audiences:

> My name is Daffy Duck,
> I worked on a Merry-Go-Round,
> The job was swell
> I did quite well
> Till the Merry-Go-Round broke down.
> (Who-hoo! Who-hoo! Who-hoo! Who-hoo!)
> The guy that worked with me,
> Was a horse with a lavender eye,
> Around in whirls, we winked at girls
> Till the Merry-Go-Round broke down.
> (plays flute)
> Up and down and round we sped,
> That dizzy pace soon went to my head,
> Now you know why I'm dizzy
> And do the things I do
> I am askew [or "a screw"] and you'd be too
> If the Merry-Go-Round broke down.
> (Who-hoo! Who-hoo! Who-hoo-who-hoo-who-hoo-who-hoo!)

Throughout the cartoon, Egghead finds he is no match for Daffy who is wild and unruly and hops and "Who-hoos!" like a crazy fool all over the place. At every turn, Daffy bests him until Egghead finally succeeds in knocking out Daffy and netting him. Ready to celebrate, a duck from a mental ward suddenly appears out of nowhere to claim Daffy and haul him off to the nearest mental hospital. Instead, the other duck and Daffy turn the tables on Egghead and beat him up. Fed up, Egghead figures if he can't beat 'em, he'll join 'em. So together they hop and "Who-hoo! Who-hoo!" into the distance as the iris fades out.

In *Daffy Duck and Egghead* and other films throughout this period, Tex continued to demonstrate his unique, freewheeling style of humor while firmly entrenching himself as a modern-day parodist by mocking everything in sight: travelogues, documentaries, classic nursery rhymes, popular fairy tales, and Western lore, a theme he would later carry with him when moving over to MGM.

FINDING HUMOR IN THE ABSURD

By far Tex's favorite target at Warner Bros. were those uninspired studio travelogue and documentary films featuring the arrogant off-camera narrator describing for audiences the splendid sights and sounds. He found his niche, mercilessly churning out an entire series of mock-documentaries and pseudo-travelogues—including *Detouring America, Cross Country Detours, Aviation Vacation, Crazy Cruise*, and others—that reminded audiences of another popular live-action, short-subject comedy series of that era, the MGM *Pete Smith Specialties*: The narration was done straight to contrast the strangely humorous subject matter and corny gags in the animated vignettes.

The Isle of Pingo Pongo set the stage for his standout effort, *Detouring America*, released on August 26, 1939. Nominated that year for an Academy Award, Tex again spoofs the James Fitzpatrick–MGM *Traveltalks* shorts, using a myriad of gags to poke fun at the popular live-action series and an off-camera narrator to bridge the comedy material and set up a comical ending. This time as the narrator intones, "As we fly off into the sunset we bid you a good night," the sun suddenly plunges from the sky before the narrator finishes his usual pitch. A more sadistic gag features a "human fly" climbing up the side of one of New York's tallest buildings, only to plummet to his death, screaming and all. The *Motion Picture Herald*, a Hollywood trade journal, reviewed the film as "one of the better and more amusing in the Merrie Melodies series."

Another amusing effort was his 1939 *Merrie Melodies* cartoon, *Land of the Midnight Fun*. Written by Melvin Millar and narrated by Robert C. Bruce, the film is a capitulation of spot gags shaped around the premise of a cruise to Nome, Alaska, including the many sights and sounds—a penguin eating two fish, suddenly devoured by larger fish; two Eskimos preparing to rub noses, with the woman applying "lipstick" to her nose first; and a "timber" wolf alternately crying, "Timber!" with the joke being on the audience.

Besides being wildly entertaining, Tex's cartoon travelogues were also innovative. He was the first animator to use oil-painted backgrounds in his cartoons. One reason was to save time and costs because, as he once stated, "The guy could work faster in oils, and his color was more vivid." He employed this new technique in the *Merrie Melodies* travelogue comedy, *Cross Country Detours* (1940). Throughout the one-reel short, he developed a running gag of a dog running wildly through the forest, shouting gleefully, "Trees, trees, trees! And mine, all mine!" For the scene, Tex had his background artist Johnny Rushmore paint the background all in oils, including the Rushmore memorial named after the artist. Later, when Tex joined Metro-Goldwyn-Mayer's cartoon department, he took Rushmore with him and had Rushmore do watercolor backgrounds and oils that were "more stylized."

Tex likewise set his sights on famous Hollywood celebrities, many right from the Warner Bros. lot, as stars of the studio's full-length feature films, parodying them in entertaining fashion in many *Merrie Melodies* cartoons that he directed. One classic example that transcended the normal conventions of seven-minute cartoons, Tex Avery-style, was *Penguin Parade* (1938). The film stars three crooning penguins—one of them a scat-singing Bing Crosby—at the grand opening of The Club Iceberg. In keeping with Tex's technique of including the audience in on his jokes, at one point in the cartoon, the penguins suddenly stop warbling long enough to "make horrible faces" at the audience before blithely continuing like nothing ever happened.

For the same film, Tex also Rotoscoped footage of a real-life stripper he shot on the studio lot and animated her into a lizard girl who

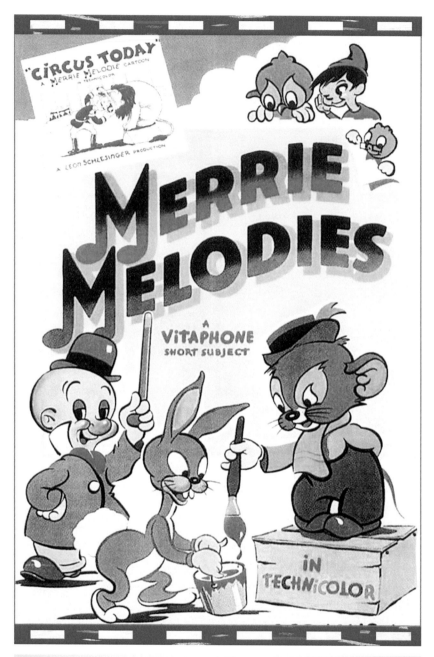

Typical of Avery's gag-ridden cartoons at Warner Bros. was his hilarious take on life under the Big Top in the *Merrie Melodies* cartoon, *Circus Today* (1940). *Courtesy MovieGoods. © Warner Bros.*

does a striptease for laughs. Only she bears lighter green skin under the skin she strips off, with the narrator commenting straight-faced, "Of course you all know that a lizard changes it skin once a year."

In *Thugs with Dirty Mugs* (1939), Tex makes a mockery of live-action gangster and crime thrillers—in particular those made by Warner Bros.—casting Edward G. Robinson as a dog-faced mobster, who holds up a phone booth by sticking his pistol into the cone-shaped mouthpiece and spouting, "Operator, this is a stickup!" and, later after being incarcerated, is forced to write on a blackboard 100 times, "I've been a naughty boy." Tex masterfully relies on film noir methods—popularized in gangster and crime thrillers of the era—such as eyewitnesses drawn in "full-shadowed outlines" and "shadow character" silhouettes of an audience member (a Rotoscoped version of Warner Bros. story man Tedd Pierce).

Off screen, Tex was just as mischievous as his onscreen characters. Schlesinger loved to gamble. So on Thursdays, payday, Avery, Robert McKimson, Friz Freleng, Hendy Bender, Schlesinger's assistant, and production manager and Schlesinger's brother-in-law Ray Katz would cash their checks and at five o'clock every Thursday night, Schlesinger would call them into his lush office to play "cutthroat poker" at a dollar a chip. "You had to go in there whether you wanted to or not," Tex later said. Many times players would bet $25 and lose or win $125 that week.

One time Tex lost $10 to Schlesinger, but he got the best of him. He paid Schlesinger all in *pennies*—1,000 of them—in a brown paper bag and said, when handing it to him, "Here's the ten I owe you, Leon." He then opened the bag and poured out all the pennies, unrolled, onto Schlesinger's desk. It took five hours afterward for Schlesinger's secretary to roll the 1,000 pennies in paper sleeves.

When Tex asked Schlesinger for a $25 dollar raise six months before he was eligible, he retorted, "Well, Tex, what I'll do, I'll get the cards out. I'll cut you high card, for fifty dollars or nothing. If you lose, you won't get another dime for a year." Tex called his bluff and played. Showing their cards, Schlesinger had an eight and Tex a jack. Schlesinger lost and buzzed his secretary and told her to tear up Tex's contract and up his salary by $50.

Often times the pranks Tex and others played on each other ended up in their cartoons. One time the mail boy made a firecracker out of cardboard, which he had the ink and painting department paint red with a fuse on top, and then tossed it into the gag room where Friz Freleng and his story man Tedd Pierce were meeting. It scared them before they learned it was fake. The next time, however, the firecracker would be real.

As Tex admitted, "Like the firecracker, we would work that: a fake and a fake, and the fuse goes out, and third one's real. Bam!" They would then put that joke in their cartoons.

Schlesinger was mostly a hands-off boss who knew nothing about animation and rarely interfered with the creative process. Longtime Warner Bros. story man Michael Maltese once said Schlesinger had "brains enough" to stay away and go on his yacht. After he came back from his seaside sojourns, Schlesinger, who spoke in a lisp, would stop in the story department and say, "Whatth cookin'?" As he often said, "Disney can make the chicken salad...I'll make money."

Tex experienced his share of difficulties working for Schlesinger, who he called "a good boss," but Schlesinger was tight with the purse strings. Oftentimes Schlesinger was unaware of what cartoons he and his fellow animators were making until he saw the rough cut of the film. Occasionally he would ask, "What are you doing?

Tex would tell him and usually he would say, "Fine," and walk away.

After Schlesinger watched the rough cut, his comments varied depending on whether he liked the film or not. Either he would say, "Gee, that's great!" if he loved the film, or "Don't give me one like that any more," if he didn't like it.

The magic and mastery of Tex is that he stayed true to himself and his convictions. He was one cartoon maverick whose elaborate themes and humors energized and entertained filmgoers—and himself—and would not stand for it to be any other way.

Falling Off a Cartoon Cliff

I n spite of his modest demeanor, personally, Tex was a shy and hard man to know. Professionally, he was vastly insecure and "worried and suffered," as he once said, to make each cartoon as great as the next, and operated under the belief that they were "never good enough" for him.

Former Warner Bros. director and colleague Friz Freleng called Tex "the most insecure director I'd ever seen at the time. Always afraid of being fired." With fear as a driving force, Tex routinely carried a timing chart with him anytime he left his desk so when he ran into Schlesinger it would look like "he was working."

As a result, Tex never took his position or status in the industry for granted. He was always toiling to make his next cartoon better than his last. Despite his success at Warner Bros., not even story man Michael Maltese could convince his colleague that he could relax.

During a conversation, Maltese said to him, "You proved yourself already."

"No," Tex responded, "it's [his cartoons] got to be better."

Tex was intent on making "funny pictures" and abided by one simple philosophy: "I tried to do something I thought I would laugh at if I were to see it on the screen, rather than worry about 'Will a ten-year-old laugh at this?'"

45

Tex and his Warner Bros. colleagues knew "we couldn't top Disney." Instead, they understood that their cartoons appealed to kids and adults, and they created cartoons with characters and storylines that were more sophisticated, more grown-up, more anarchic, and wilder and funnier than Disney's.

Throughout 1940, Tex kept up his no-holds-barred assault on the animation world and ratcheted up the topical and wartime humor in his films. One such effort was *Ceiling Hero*. This outlandish *Merrie Melodies* cartoon parodies the "latest developments in science of modern aviation" and air travel through a series of blackout gags (a series of rapid-fire gags in succession): a six-propeller plane whose wing flies by itself; a pilot parachuting out of the plane with a parachute that reads, "Good to the last drop"; an exploding rocket that is launched that says, "Eat at Tony's," and more.

In *Holiday Highlights*, another *Merrie Melodies* cartoon released that year, Tex puts a humorous spotlight in this pictorial calendar of traditional American holidays, including New Year's, Valentine's Day, Washington's Birthday, April Fool's Day, Mother's Day, Thanksgiving, and Christmas in a series of spot gags: the father of a young George Washington, asking if he chopped down the cherry tree, to which George replies, "Hmmm....Couldst be!"; for April Fool's Day, a blank page of the calendar with the narrator giggling out of control and a theater management slide suddenly appearing on the screen that says: "T'aint Funny, McGee!"; for Halloween, a witch flying on a broom with a banner attached advertising: "Dollar Days."

Another *Merrie Melodies* cartoon that Tex directed, *Of Fox and Hounds*, captures the mirth and madness of hunting, with him absurdly paying homage to author John Steinbeck's mentally-challenged strong man Lenny from Steinbeck's famous novel *Of Mice and Men*. Only Tex casts him as a dim-witted St. Bernard, Willoughby, whose job is to hunt and catch a wily fox named George (also named after the quick-witted character in Steinbeck's novel). Willoughby, however, is so dumb that he does not know George is a fox and when he sees him, asks, "Which way did they go? Do you know where the fox is?"

George slyly gives him directions and says, "You can't miss him!"

Tex's affection for Steinbeck's characters continued even after he left Warner Bros. and went on to MGM, where he created the characters George and Junior, inspired by Steinbeck's fictional work.

WHADDYA KNOW, DOC—A RABBIT!

That summer, Tex also ushered into movie theaters a new character that marked yet another landmark achievement in his career, while unknowingly creating what would become the studio's biggest cartoon star of all time.

In the late 1930s, Schlesinger directors Ben Hardaway and Cal Dalton introduced an unnamed squat, slender-eared, and cotton-tailed rabbit, like Daffy Duck in a "rabbit suit," with a speeded-up voice and cackle reminiscent of Walter Lantz's famous character Woody Woodpecker, in three *Looney Tunes* cartoons: *Porky's Hare Hunt* (1938), directed by Hardaway, *Hare-Um Scare-Um* (1939), co-directed by Hardaway and Dalton, and *Elmer's Candid Camera* (1940), helmed by Chuck Jones featuring a considerably toned down prototype of Hardaway and Dalton's version and the first cartoon to mark the appearance of Elmer Fudd evolved from Tex's Egghead character.

Though the rabbit character enjoying varying degrees of success, as Joe Adamson writes in his book *Tex Avery: King of Cartoons*, Hardaway and Dalton had "managed to misdirect the character so thoroughly that he was more annoying to the audience than he was to his antagonist."

A year after the last experimentation, Tex took a stab at overhauling the rabbit character. He told character designer Robert Givens, after reviewing Charlie Thorson's original model sheet of the rabbit, that it "didn't have any personality, and was too cute." So Tex redesigned him into, as he once described, "a street-smart wise ass of the first order" and "certified screwy rabbit," doing most of the drawings himself and assigning Givens to draw an updated model sheet of the character that was "hepper and more clever, with a snappier smile and devilish eyes." Tex entirely changed the character's mental and physical characteristics, making him brainier, brasher, more irreverent, and more deliberate and composed, defusing any harm that comes his way and exhausting the patience of his aggressor by nonchalantly chewing on his carrot. Tex's addition of these distinctive characteristics—complemented by the Brooklynese of voice-artist Mel Blanc—marked the birth of Bugs Bunny.

Bugs' original screen character in the earlier Hardaway and Dalton cartoons was far too obnoxious and unlikeable. In some respects, Bugs Bunny's original characterization in the earlier films resembled Walt Disney's cartoon luminary, Max Hare, who debuted in the Disney *Silly Symphony* cartoon *The Tortoise and the Hare* (1935), which won an Academy Award. When Tex took over Bugs, he modified his character by giving him a personality that was more like that of comedian Groucho Marx, yet with the subtleness of Marx and traits that were far more accepted by moviegoers than the hopping lunatic he portrayed in earlier cartoons.

Tex unleashed his latest creation in his fifth cartoon of 1940, *A Wild Hare*, the first "official" Bugs Bunny cartoon, released on July 27. The color one-reel short established the basic formula and character precepts and nuances—and classic catchline—successfully mined thereafter by other Warner Bros. directors. To wit: a gullible half-wit hunter (Elmer J. Fudd) hunting for "wabbits" and presumably catching one, a cool, cagey rabbit who steers the barrel of his shotgun away from his face with his white-gloved hand and then shrewdly disarms the hunter by matter-of-factly chomping a carrot and dauntlessly inquiring, "Eh, What's up, Doc?" The pairing marked the beginning of an onscreen rivalry that would produce gales of laughter from theater audiences, and large profits from their films for Warner's. (The film originally included a joke about actress Carole Lombard but after she died in a tragic plane crash in January 1942, the joke, considered in "poor taste," was replaced by substituting actress Barbara Stanwyck in Lombard's place.)

In developing *A Wild Hare*, Tex determined that Bugs needed a "human foil" for the cartoon to work and settled on the chubby Elmer Fudd. "We didn't feel that we had anything until we got it on the screen and it got quite a few laughs," he told author Joe Adamson.

Tex ran with the idea after previewing the cartoon and receiving glowing praise from theater exhibitors and from Leon Schlesinger, who enthused, "Boy, give us as many of those as you can!"

Tex Avery's Bugs Bunny squares off for the first time with the befuddled hunter Elmer Fudd in Avery's first Oscar-nominated short, *A Wild Hare* (1940). © *Warner Bros.*

Tex defined Bugs Bunny's success this way: "He was a smart-aleck, but he was casual about it. The opening line in the first one [*A Wild Hare*] was 'Eh, What's up, Doc?' And, gee, it floored 'em! They expected the rabbit to scream, or anything but make a casual remark—here's a guy with a gun in his face! It got such a laugh that we said, 'Boy, we'll do that every chance we get.'"

Tex was responsible for creating Bugs' now familiar refrain, "What's up, Doc?" Remembering his Texas youth, he fondly recalled how, during his days in high school, people would call each other "Doc," and that the phrase became an extension of other lines people commonly used on the street, like "Hey, Doc! Whaddya know!", "What's up, Doc?", or "How ya been today, Doc?" When he came to California, he would use those same slang phrases in the daily course of his conversation and people would ask him, "Where do you get that 'Doc' stuff?" In developing Bugs for *A Wild Hare*, his idea for the catchphrase for Bugs just clicked.

When it came to naming Bugs, Tex and Schlesinger did not see eye to eye on the subject and clashed over what to call the character. Originally he wanted to dub his creation Jack Rabbit or Jack E. Rabbit. As he told author Joe Adamson, "I thought it would please my Texas friends." The name Bugs Bunny won out, mostly because the name was catchier, like those of the studio's other stars, Porky Pig and Daffy Duck.

In the years after Tex's film debut of Bugs, many other directors at Warner Bros. tried taking credit for creating the character. Before Schlesinger died, he credited Tex as Bugs' creator since it was he who gave Bugs his distinctive devil-may-care personality, which changed, with some exceptions, under the helm of directors Friz Freleng, Robert McKimson, and Chuck Jones, into more of a counterrevolutionary. Certainly, Ben Hardaway deserves credit for developing a more crudely, unruly, and unnamed rabbit that was the predecessor to Tex's creation. And while controversy has reined for years on the subject of Bugs' creation, Tex is the one man who gave life to the Bugs Bunny that audiences would love and remember for generations to come and would become the studio's biggest star of all time.

Michael Maltese, who was a contributing gag writer on the cartoon and later chief story man/collaborator for director Chuck Jones, said of Tex's Bugs Bunny in an interview with author Joe Adamson: "The guy with the most mischievous Bugs Bunny character in the whole studio was Tex Avery...And you can put this down—I don't care what you hear from anybody else—he took Bugs Bunny and instilled into him the character that made Bugs Bunny...When Avery was gone, the heritage that was left to us at Warner's was Bugs Bunny, Daffy Duck, and Porky Pig. And it was up to us to develop these characters and turn them into something."

For Tex, *A Wild Hare* represented a major milestone in his career. The cartoon was nominated for an Academy Award for "Best Short-Subject," and, though it lost to MGM's Hugh Harman one-reeler *The Milky Way,* being nominated twice in two years for the prestigious honor enhanced Tex's stature at the studio and within the animation industry.

Tex went on to direct a menagerie of *Merrie Melodies* cartoons the following year, mostly spot-gag shorts such as *The Crackpot Quail, Haunted Mouse, Hollywood Steps Out, The Bug Parade,* and his last Porky Pig and final *Looney Tunes* cartoon, *Porky's Preview.*

Despite the success of his first Bugs Bunny cartoon, *A Wild Hare,* sadly Tex only directed two more before leaving the studio. His second was the *Merrie Melodies* short *Tortoise Beats Hare* (1941), a parody of the Aesop fable *The Tortoise and the Hare* and the 1934 Disney *Silly Symphony* cartoon *The Tortoise and the Hare.* Released to theaters on March 15, 1941, Tex's inventiveness is on display right from the opening credits as Bugs nonchalantly wanders out, alternately munching on his carrot while grossly mispronouncing the names of the Warner Bros. staffers in the credits as they roll by him—"Menahenn" for story man Dave Monahan," "Mac-Emson" for animator Charles McKimson, and "Avary" for director Tex Avery. Introducing a new character, Cecil the Turtle, Bugs bets the sleepy-eyed turtle $10 that he can beat him in a race, and the dour-faced Cecil happily accepts.

The slow-moving Cecil is no fool, however. After the race begins and Bugs gets a huge head start, Cecil calls upon his cousin Chester Turtle and his eight other cousins, who sound and look just like him, to take turns showing up at different points in the race just when Bugs thinks he has victory at hand. As Cecil dryly says to the audience, "We do this stuff to him all through the picture!"

Just as Bugs crosses the finish line and thinks he has won, standing on the other side is one of Cecil's kin claiming victory and demanding his prize money. The cartoon ends with Bugs wondering if he has been duped when all 10 turtles reply at once, "Hmmm…eh, it's a possibility!"

One complaint Tex had in directing cartoons at Warner Bros. and later at MGM was how he and his fellow directors were credited on screen as "Supervision by" instead of receiving director's credit.

Many times reviewers would fail to mention the director of the cartoon in their review, or when they did, they would give scant mention. Of course, Tex believed the way the system worked was intentionally against them, because the studio feared if the directors were mentioned in good reviews, then they would want a raise. Studios also feared that many would join the Directors Guild, a union, if they were credited as directors, but finally relented and gave animators director credit after the guild disallowed them to join.

BREAKING OUT OF THE CARTOON ASYLUM

Tex never lost a desire to break into doing live-action films, an interest that developed during his time at Universal and continued during his stay at Warner Bros. and later MGM. In the summer of 1941, he developed an idea that he was sure would usher him in that direction: a revolutionary series of live-action shorts with wisecracking "talking animals" as the main characters. In the films, animals would speak— thanks to animation. Animated mouths were double exposed over the live footage of the animals, creating a believable illusion that animals could talk. He made a film test of the idea and also wrote a script for the pilot and showed it to his boss Leon Schlesinger, who told Tex to present his idea to Gordon Hollingshead, head of Warner Bros. live-action short subject department. Hollingshead loved it and said, "Sure, we'll make one. Make a pilot."

Afterward, Tex met again with Schlesinger to tell him the news, and said, "I'll make a pilot over the weekends. Get a camera and we'll shoot zoos and animals." But Schlesinger balked. "No, I'll pay you for your scripts and gags," he said, "and we'll let Warner's (Hollingshead's department) do the films, because we're in the business of making cartoons."

The headstrong Tex argued that he wanted to produce the series himself. Schlesinger wouldn't budge. He said he could not agree to such terms. He would either have total control, or nothing. Tex lost his temper. A heated argument ensued. Finally, as punishment, Schlesinger laid him off for eight weeks.

During his layoff, Tex took his "talking animals" proposal else-where, to his good friends Bob Carlysle and Jerry Fairbanks, producers of *Odd Occupations* shorts for Paramount. He had met them years earlier at Universal, when he was on staff at the Lantz studio. He met with Carlysle and presented his idea to him. Carlysle thought the premise was fantastic, so fantastic that they shot a test reel using stock footage of a desert horn toad with Tex animating one line of dialogue mouthed by the toad: "I don't care what you say, I'm horny." They showed the footage and script to the powers-that-be at Paramount, who immediately financed the production of a large-scale, short-short series, based on Tex's concept, called *Speaking of Animals*.

Paramount Pictures' *Speaking of Animals* series employed then cutting-edge special effects to achieve Tex's vision of animals that could talk, sing, and fire off comedy one-liners. Fairbanks employed the rather tedious and laborious system of rear-projection and Rotoscoping to replace the animals' mouths with realistically animated human ones and dubbing in the voices. As he once recalled, "We would film live actors such as Mel Blanc and Sterling Holloway in black face with their lips painted white. That way, we could have just their lip movements visible on film. The images were then traced frame by frame, reshot as animation that in turn was matted into the actual animal footage."

The shorts became so popular with audiences that they were simultaneously booked with many of Paramount Pictures' major feature film releases and advertised on theater marquees along with the main feature, not something common with short subjects.

Tex's deal with Carlysle and Fairbanks entitled him to a financial stake in the production, but Tex had a falling out with them over money after directing two films—*Down on the Farm*, which was nominated for an Oscar for "Best Short Subject" in 1942, and *In the Zoo*. As Tex stated, "I had a deal with the boys, and there again I felt that I was entitled to a little money. We had a falling out and I sold out my portion to Fairbanks."

Tex later regretted his decision. The series was largely successful, lasting eight years, and won an Academy Award in 1943 for "Best Short Subject."

After returning to Warner Bros., Tex went back to directing. He finished helming his third cartoon and Warner's fifth that season, *The Heckling Hare*, starring Bugs Bunny. In this short, Bugs was paired with the adversarial Willoughby the Dog, who is hunting Bugs. The cartoon builds to a long climax of Bugs and Willoughby accidentally falling off a cliff and free-falling through the sky until they land safely on the ground. Comically turning to the audience, Bugs says, "Fooled ya, didn't we?"

Bugs and Willoughby then repeat the same stunt: They walk off another cliff, but before they do, Bugs turns to the audience and says: "Hold on to your hats, folks. Here we go again!" As they plummet below, the scene fades out as the familiar "That's, All Folks!" end title splashes across the screen.

At the end of the film, Tex originally planned to have Bugs and Willoughby fall off the cliff *three* times to milk the most laughs out of the gag. Apparently, only he saw the humor in it. Reportedly Schlesinger, who approved the ending, screened the cartoon for studio head Jack Warner prior to its release. Warner supposedly disliked the ending, particularly the line, "Hold on to your hats!" that referenced a risqué joke that was popular at the time, and the idea of his studio's biggest cartoon star "falling to an uncertain fate." As a result, Warner allegedly ordered that Schlesinger change the ending.

Schlesinger immediately met with Tex. A quarrel erupted between them. Tex would not compromise his artistic principles. He saw nothing wrong with the scene. He vehemently refused to change it. Rather than bow to pressure and give Warner and Schlesinger what they wanted, Tex walked out of the studio.

Schlesinger slapped Tex with a six-week suspension. In the meantime, instead of appointing another director to complete the film, Schlesinger changed the ending himself. He cut the final 60 feet of film from the original print to Bugs and Willoughby falling off the cliff only *once*, ending with them putting "on the brakes" and making a soft, feet-first landing as Bugs says, "N'yah, fooled ya, didn't we!" and Willoughby agrees, "Yeah!" before the cartoon quickly fades to black. (In television versions broadcast on TBS, TNT, Cartoon Network, and Boomerang,

Willoughby's final line and the fade-out are cut from the prints to cover up Schlesinger's abrupt ending in the original print.)

While Tex was suspended, Schlesinger released his version of *The Heckling Hare* to theaters along with Tex's *Merrie Melodies* cartoon *Aviation Vacation*, with no director credit for him. That September, Schlesinger released his final directed Bugs Bunny short—again without naming Tex in the credits—*All This and Rabbit Stew.*

In September 1941, Tex quit his position at Warner Bros. Schlesinger appointed Avery protégé Bob Clampett from animator to director to take over his unit. In many ways, fate stepped in at the right time. Tex needed a change of environment. Some of the 33-year-old animator's best work was still ahead, taking his frenetically paced and highly exaggerated humor to new levels of lunacy.

5

Roaring Back at MGM

Fortunately, Tex was soon back to work in animation. He joined the cartoon department at Metro-Goldwyn-Mayer, better known as MGM, as a unit director, replacing veteran directors Hugh Harman and Rudolf Ising, producers of independent cartoons released through Metro before the formation of the studio's cartoon division. Although Tex has said he made the decision on his own, in recent years it was learned that his old Warner Brothers friend, Friz Freleng, was also partly responsible for his new job.

Freleng remembers: "I told Tex that I thought they [MGM] would be happier if he desired to direct there, never dreaming that he would consider applying. He told me later that he certainly regretted his decision to leave Leon and go to MGM. But once on the job, he stuck it out, until the demise of the cartoon studio."

Animator and collaborator Michael Lah felt that Tex did his best work after moving to Metro. "When Tex moved in, it was like an avalanche hit."

In 14 years at Metro, Tex would incite more moments of comical lunacy on the screen, directing 67 cartoons shorts, many among the studio's most memorable, and creating a maniacal menagerie of characters—

56

Avery poses for a publicity shot shortly after joining MGM in September 1941.

Droopy, George and Junior, and Screwy Squirrel—to keep up his frenzied comic assault on audiences.

From the moment he set foot on the Metro lot, Tex found the atmosphere within the studio's cartoon department "very competitive," with the department split into two units—one headed by the studio's so-called "darlings" William Hanna and Joseph Barbera, directors of the studio's Oscar-winning *Tom and Jerry* cartoon series, and another by Tex, whose team of animators included Ray Abrams, Irv Spence, Preston Blair, and Ed Love. His new boss, MGM's cartoon division head Fred Quimby, was strictly a businessman who had no understanding what-soever of storylines or gags or the elements necessary to produce a good cartoon and "wasn't easy to get along with." As Tex said, "There you had to fight for what you thought was right."

Nonetheless, coming to Metro at the time was the best decision Tex ever made. The change of environment gave him the opportunity to direct films that were wilder, more outlandish, more outrageous, and more unrestrained. They were punctuated by hilarious sight gags and visual puns that spun off each other in a frenetically paced cascade of humor with sheer energy and laugh-getting power that rarely slackened. Furthermore, Tex expanded on his use of conventions and devices, for which he barely tapped the surface at Warner Bros., taking his characters and films to higher levels of absurdity and extremes.

Tex gave audiences a taste of his iconoclastic humor right away with his second-directed cartoon—but first released under his new studio banner—*Blitz Wolf*. Released on August 22, 1942, the exuber-ant, briskly paced and gag-filled wartime parody takes a new spin on the classic nursery rhyme the *Three Little Pigs*. In this "pro-democ-racy propaganda" war effort, the Pigs aren't anything like the nursery rhyme: One is an Army sergeant who lives in a brick-and-armor-plated fortress while the other two pigs have become lazy isolation-ists. Banding together, they use a cavalcade of armory and weapons to thwart the mustachioed Adolf Wolf, dressed like Germany's Adolf Hitler, who fails in his assault on the three pigs after storming into the picture. (Incidentally, the film marked the first appearance of Tex's Wolf character that would appear, in some form, in many Avery-directed MGM shorts). *Box Office Magazine*, in reviewing the

The big bad wolf and the three pigs are shown in a poster for Avery's wartime send-up, the Oscar-nominated MGM short *Blitz Wolf* (1942). © *Metro-Goldwyn-Mayer.*

film, raved: "They don't come any better. Audiences, recovering from their laughter, will stand up and cheer for this one. Tex Avery, who directed, is a man to watch."

The Hollywood film community apparently took notice as well. Tex's MGM cartoon was nominated in 1943 by members for the Academy of Motion Picture Arts and Sciences for an Oscar for "Best Short Subject," his third such nomination in his career. Unfortunately, he lost the award that year to a similar war-themed effort, Walt Disney's *Der Fuehrer's Face* starring Donald Duck.

Seven days after *Blitz Wolf*, theatergoers were treated to Tex's first MGM cartoon short released out of order, *The Early Bird Dood It*. The plotline involves something familiar from his Warner Bros. days: a cartoon chase story involving a bird, worm, and cat in that order. The film features an early bird, carrying a "Worm Ration Book," in pursuit of a Lou Costello sound-a-like worm. The worm allies himself with the cat but is ultimately caught and eaten by the bird, but there is a twist: The cat then devours the bird. In typical Avery style, a sign suddenly appears in jest at the end saying, "Sad ending, isn't it?"

DROLLING FOR LAUGHS WITH DROOPY

While studio colleagues Hanna and Barbera had already established themselves by directing their own "chase" cartoon series in Tom and Jerry, the studio's biggest stars to date, Tex soon countered with his original creation: a dour bloodhound Droopy, named Happy Hound in his first film (even though on model sheets for his first cartoon the character is called "Droopy").

Happy Hound/Droopy was based on Wallace Wimple, a supporting character in radio's *The Fibber McGee and Molly Show*, played by Bill Thompson, who Avery enlisted to voice the character. Tex loved Thompson's funny, meek, "mush-mouth" character on the radio program and said, "Hell, let's put a dog to it." Fearing legal repercussions from the show's producers, Thompson created the voice but with some minor variations. (Later, voice-artist Daws Butler, best known as the voice of TV's Huckleberry Hound and others, assumed the role and did the voice of Droopy by literally "squeezing his cheeks" together, as did Don Messick, who succeeded Butler.)

Introduced in the March 1943 cartoon *Dumb-Hounded*, Happy Hound stars as a police dog trying to recapture the Wolf, who breaks out of Swing-Swing Prison (and has a reward of $5,000 or "one pound of coffee") and goes to extraordinary lengths to elude the pint-sized hound who pops up at every place he finds shelter. The plot becomes the basis for a great running gag, one that only Happy Hound plays for laughs. Even though the gag was originally used in his 1941 Bugs Bunny cartoon *Tortoise Beats Hare,* Tex reworked it to the point where it is better than the original. Every time Happy Hound catches up with the Wolf, he tells him, "Now promise me you won't move." Of course, the Wolf never keeps his promises (what Wolf would?); he trots off to find a new hiding place. There, waiting for the Wolf is, of course, Happy Hound, who manages to say drolly: "You moved!" The gag repeats itself until it builds to a hilarious climax. Tex later expanded the gag in a similar Droopy cartoon, *Northwest Hounded Police* (1946).

Happy Hound was an immediate hit with critics and filmgoers and, as Droopy, would become the studio's next biggest star after Hanna-Barbera's Tom and Jerry. Tex succeeded, in part, due to a basic formula he established in the first cartoon that he repeated throughout the series: the big guy versus little guy premise exaggerated to epic proportions. Although his dwarfed size and Buster Keaton–like deadpan made him appear humble and innocent, Droopy was hardly a pushover. He thwarted his adversary—usually Tex's stock-in-trade nemesis, the Wolf—with a sudden burst of brute strength that belied his size—in a "survival of the fittest" (a theme Tex used in all of the Droopy films) to emerge victorious.

Developing ideas and stories for his cartoons at Metro was a true collaboration between Tex and his story man Heck Allen. Allen was a successful fiction writer turned story man who authored more than 30 Western novels. He joined MGM's cartoon unit in 1937 and served as Tex's story man on many of his cartoons at Metro and, in Tex's words, "was a good man to have around. He was the best gag man I ever worked with." Like many of Tex's other colleagues, Allen knew little about him.

Avery's first starring character at MGM, Droopy (originally named "Happy Hound"), and his archrival, the Wolf, are shown in the original model sheet for the first Droopy cartoon, *Dumb-Hounded* (1943). © *Metro-Goldwyn-Mayer.*

He called Tex "a loner, right down to his last gasp." However, in working with the exceptionally gifted animator and director, Allen observed him to be "a generous, warm man: who was enthusiastic and liked people but was also sensitive."

Allen's strength was story (Tex credited him with helping him "a lot" in this area), whereas gags were Tex's territory. He would come up with a joke, Allen with a situation, and things would steamroll from there. Sometimes they would get stuck and table the idea for a while and come back to solve it later. "I never had any set way of building a story," Tex admitted. "Sometimes we'd go back over our notes and find an idea that had a good beginning and no ending, and we'd finally solve it."

Allen developed a strong bond with Tex, distinguished by similar upbringings—both were born and raised in small, rural hometowns and amused each other with tales of Taylor, Texas, and Jackson County, Missouri, Allen's birthplace—and their love for Western culture and sharing the same sense of humor. As Allen put it, "He was the funniest sonabitch that ever lived."

The pacing of Tex's cartoons at Metro would become more frenetic—for a very good reason: He discovered by cutting scenes tighter—to around eight feet per gag—his films were "funnier" and he was able to double his quotient of humor by loading up his films with even more gags. The story, though it served a vital purpose to thread together the gags, was secondary. His characters would get smashed by a falling anvil and then take another step, only to suddenly fall into a well, with the mayhem building from there. Of the furiously quick pacing of his cartoons at Metro, Tex said, "Put all my cartoons together and start running 'em and, well, it looks like speeded up film. You run the old stuff (I still call my stuff 'new'), and they would take thirty feet of film to do a gag."

Following the outbreak of World War II, involving the mobilization of more than 100 million military personnel from many nations and becoming the deadliest conflict in history, patriotism soared across the country. Such fervor was not lost on Hollywood studios that supported the war effort by producing propaganda and training films. Many training films produced for American servicemen were animated at studios like Warner Bros. and MGM. Actual servicemen were given deferments and were featured in these films. In addition to producing theatrical cartoon shorts, Metro also produced training films for the Army and Navy.

Swept up in the patriotism of the times, Tex directed a handful of shorts, interjecting much humor while often addressing serious subjects, to train American servicemen, and created a new character in one of the films: a red-lipped beauty with long eyelashes, Bertie the Bomber, used to show servicemen how to load a bomber. Often Tex's gag men came up with gags after consulting with an Army sergeant involved in the making of the films and who Avery called "a good audience."

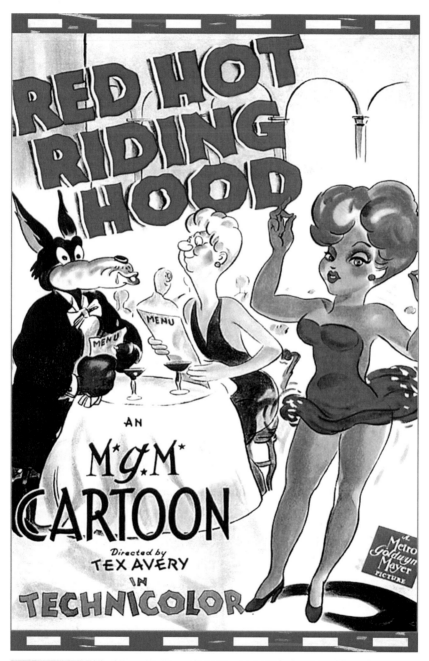

Saucy Red with the lascivious Wolf as featured on the theatrical
one-sheet for *Red Hot Riding Hood* (1943). *Courtesy MovieGoods.* ©
Metro-Goldwyn-Mayer.

FRACTURED FAIRYTALES, OUTRAGEOUS PARODIES, AND A GIRL NAMED RED

It was during such uncertain times, with a country at war and millions of Americans confronted with government-mandated rationing of food, gas, and clothing to avoid widespread shortages, that Tex directed his most celebrated "fractured fairy tale:" *Red Hot Riding Hood.*

Released to theaters on May 8, 1943, the film took on a subject—and theme in a series of spoofs to come—that was taboo in this era of innocence: sex. The film caused quite a stir by spoofing—and making a sex object of—the classic nursery rhyme character Little Red Riding Hood. Tex cast Red as a sexy hot vamp with short, attractive legs and sexy-looking eyes opposite an overstimulated, wildly gyrating Wolf, depicting the "libidinous frustrations of males everywhere." Red, strutting her stuff in lovingly animated song-and-dance numbers, sends the Wolf into a comic frenzy. His eyes pop out of their sockets on springs. He pounds his head with a sledgehammer. He lights his nose, thinking it is a cigarette. In general, he acts like a lasciviously demented fool in Red's presence. Though Tex's Red never acted lewd, division head Quimby, in no laughing mood, was "horrified" at first over the idea, until eventually getting on board.

The idea originated while Tex was producing Army training films. He completed cutting and dubbing the first cut of *Red Hot Riding Hood* and previewed the film in a projection room at Metro. Among those Tex invited was the Army sergeant with whom he had consulted. The sergeant reacted uproariously to the sexually charged antics of the Wolf, including the rough-cut scene of him getting "hot" under the collar over the curvaceous dancing girl Red, a scene that ended on the cutting room floor after the Hays Office, Hollywood's censorship board, viewed the film and demanded it be removed. Tex ran into trouble as well with the Hays Office, who objected to other scenes of his "man-about-town," girl-chasing Wolf (such as when the Wolf stiffens up like an arrow and rolls out his tongue suggestively), which were cut from the final print. Word traveled fast to Washington, D.C., about the film, with studio president Louis B. Mayer being telegrammed with a request from a colonel to send prints of the "uncut" version overseas for the troops.

Tex credits animator Preston Blair, who teamed up with Avery on many of Droopy, George and Junior, and Screwball Squirrel cartoons, for creating the sultry-voiced and deliciously inviting Red—from her gaggled-up red locks to her curvy, dancer-like legs. "He wouldn't let anyone touch her! He did all the girl sequences," Tex later commented.

As a consequence of federally mandated gas rationing under way to conserve fuel to aid the war effort, carpooling was quite common then. Of those in their MGM's animation group, Tex and Bill Hanna were the only ones who owned cars. Alternating every other day, they carpooled to the studio, picking up as passengers writer Rick Hogan and Edna Pidgeon, actor Walter Pidgeon's daughter, who worked as an inker and painter. In Hanna's words, "Tex's backseat humor was as spontaneously zany as any of his wildest cartoons and often a lot racier." Consequently, he and Tex became close friends during their years at the studio, often going on fishing and camping trips that were "nearly as freewheeling and unpredictable as any of Avery's most outrageous cartoon creations."

In the meantime, Tex managed to find new ways to tickle audiences' funny bones. An example was *Who Killed Who?*, his fifth cartoon at Metro. In this film noir and murder mystery spoof, Tex uses a live actor at the beginning of the film to host this eight-minute dilly, and explains that the purpose of the cartoon is "to prove that crime doesn't pay." The cartoon pokes fun at practically every murder mystery cliché, prop, and device—a dark, stormy night with bolts of lightning cracking over an ominous mansion; a sage, old dog in his chair reading a book titled after the film and saying to the audience, "If this is anything like the book, I get bumped off"; and then a knife that suddenly goes screaming by, securing itself on the nearest wall, with a note attached that says: "You will die at 11:30."

The short is classic Tex Avery through and through—with a canine private detective (patterned after actor Fred Kelsey, the perennial hotel detective of 1930s and 1940s films) arriving on the scene to solve the murder and yelling to the entire household, "Don't anybody move!" A silhouetted moviegoer (a device Tex used effectively at Warner Bros.), obviously not paying attention, suddenly gets up from his seat. The detective, who quickly notices the interruption, shoots him, adding comically, "I said *nobody* move!"

Original poster for Avery's classic detective spoof, *Who Killed Who?* (1943). *Courtesy MovieGoods.* © *Metro-Goldwyn-Mayer.*

The film employs a solid array of sight gags throughout as the canine detective narrows down his list of potential killers. Panning his flashlight, he reveals a wall of paintings in a secluded back room and stops on a painting of a partially nude woman. Immediately, the inspector swings back his flashlight to find the woman now *fully* clothed. Another gag has two eyes suspiciously peering out a slot in a closet door. When the door closes on them, the eyes are separated from their owners and have to knock on the door to get in. Avery even spoofs the old murder mystery cliché: finding a bound and gagged body in the closet. But the detective finds not just one body, but *17*, with one of the cadavers stopping in mid-air as he drops like a human domino out of the closet to say to the audience, "Ah, yes. Quite a bunch of us, isn't it!"

Tex went from the sublime to the ridiculous in subsequent cartoons that year. An August release, *One Ham's Family*, was a satirical update of the classic nursery rhyme *The Three Little Pigs*, and its title parodied the popular radio show *One Man's Family*. On Christmas Eve, the hungry Wolf, as Santa Claus, who sets out to bag a ham, is outfoxed by Junior (patterned after Red Skelton's "Mean Widdle Kid"), the son of Mother and Father Pig, who is left home alone. In theaters that November, *What's Buzzin' Buzzard*, made during the country's time of war rationing, has two starving vultures (one with a mouth that has a sign reading, "Closed for the Duration"), desperate for food. After potential meals slip through their grasp, they resort to cannibalizing each other with live-action shots of a "juicy steak" intercut to tease audiences. The cartoon was Quimby's least favorite. "He darn near threw up every time he saw it," Tex said. When Tex received word that the Library of Congress was adding it to its collection of films to be preserved, Quimby was dumbstruck. He said, "Aw, they coulda picked a better one than that."

HUMORING OVER EVERYONE BUT THE BOSS

Quimby did not always appreciate or understand Tex's comic brilliance. Unlike his former boss Leon Schlesinger, who had a sense of humor, Quimby was humorless and a much tougher audience. No matter how hard Tex and his unit tried, they could never get Quimby to laugh. Tex

Tex Avery (*third from left*) shows producer Fred Quimby (*second from left*) and several guests storyboards to his first risqué romp, *Red Hot Riding Hood* (1943).

was of the belief that Quimby was too uptight about whether the films they were making were going to make money. As he stated, "You had to explain the cartoon storyboard to him in order for him to understand. We'd have the storyboard all set, and we'd show it to him and explain everything, and he'd look at it and say, 'Why does he do this?'…He couldn't understand what was so funny." Other times, Quimby would react totally opposite. He would stand there and study the storyboard several more times, shake his head, and say, "Boys…I don't like it."

Quimby's shortcomings created, at times, an atmosphere of discontent. Never having worked in animation, he had "no qualifications whatever artistically, even to sit in judgment." He fired Tex's story man, Heck Allen, seven or eight times in 12 years because he viewed him as "a trouble maker" and felt he was not contributing enough other than to "laugh at Tex's ideas," as Allen once said. But it was Tex who rehired him any time another writer wouldn't last. "I'd go home to work on the books, and pretty soon the phone would ring and I'd go back out there and have fun with Tex again," Allen recalled.

Eventually, Tex wised up. He would wait until closer to the deadline, when the cartoon he was directing was actually due for completion, before showing it to Quimby. Using a different tactic, he'd say, "Chief, this is all we've got!" and then tell his bespectacled boss that if he wanted to stop him from making the film that he would have to lay off his animators. Quimby, knowing the value of time and money, would not hear of it and would let whatever Tex was working on go through, in most cases.

While he valued the contributions of Allen and his animators, the perfectionist-driven Tex mostly succeeded by doing everything on his own. He would come up with plots and gags; draw layouts for his background artists and model sheets of the characters for his character animators; do cleanup work for their drawings; revise pages of dialogue in the script; and do some of the voices on occasion. He was really a "one-man band."

Michael Lah, who first served as an animator on Tex's *House of Tomorrow* in 1949 and later codirected with him, put it this way: "[He] would want a lot of changes. And, my gosh, even when the animation was on cels, he would cut frames on the Movieola, to get the effect he wanted."

Lah noticed, in working closely with Tex, that he was so "sensitive about failure" that he would attend public screenings of his cartoon shorts in theaters "to see how it went over."

At Metro, Tex used one model man to create all of the models and model sheets featuring every possible expression and position for each character. As he recalled, "Then I would take my roughs and give them to the animators, and they would work from the model sheets."

For every 600 feet of film—the average length of his cartoons—Tex and his staff produced around 600 drawings, sometimes more when the cartoon had two characters. That included rough sketches, positions and expressions made by his model man, and cleanup drawings by his animators made by the model man based on Tex's originals.

Tex admitted at times that he was frustrated by working as an animation director and felt he could have been more successful as a live-action film director like a Frank Capra or Frank Tashlin, who got his start in animation at Warner Bros. before directing live-action comedy features. But "Tex never understood the quality and extent of his own genius," Allen stated. "Otherwise, he would have simply picked up his briefcase, gone up on the front lot, and said, 'I'm Tex Avery. I can make the funniest goddam live-action picture you ever saw in your life, and we'll get rich together."

Instinctively, Tex had the inherent qualities to direct live-action comedy. Often, he would drop into the studio during filming of the latest Pete Smith comedy short series, and while watching them he became so intense that he would bite his nails, knowing how he could make them better. He would even go up to the director and say, "Hey, why don't you have that guy do this...." Usually, the director would laugh loudly over what Tex would suggest and Tex would give the director "five hundred dollars worth of jokes in a minute."

Tex never gave up his dream to transition into doing live-action films. One afternoon, he collaborated with Allen on a concept for a new Western comedy for comedian Red Skelton, star of such MGM features as *I Dood It* (1943) and later *The Fuller Brush Man* (1948). They developed the idea from beginning to end—the premise, the jokes, and story, but nothing ever materialized with it. It was not the first or last time Tex created ideas that ended up unproduced. He would develop many other concepts for cartoons that Quimby flatly rejected or that were never produced, including *The Big Bad Baby Sitter*, *Chicken Hearted*, *Dog's Best Friend*, *Droopy Dog Returns*, *Droopy Dog's License*, *Droopy's Serenade*, *Elephant a la King*, *Hark Hark the Bark*, and *Holland Story*.

For Tex, his dream of doing live-action features may have been grounded, but his future in animation at Metro seemed bright, for now.

6

Screwball with a Purpose

ex had a profound influence on his colleagues at Metro. His exaggerated style and irreverent humor affected his fellow animators, and that included Hanna and Barbera. As Barbera later recalled, "He (Avery) was one of the greatest, most creative cartoonists in our industry. He was a great gag man, a great story man, and he was very innovative. He was also a kind, generous man who shared his talents with everyone."

In many respects, the accelerated pace and increasingly hard-hitting gags evident in Hanna and Barbera's *Tom and Jerry* cartoons of the mid-1940s were the result of Tex's influence. Part of Tex's success, in Barbera's opinion, was his "sense of timing and his originality were brilliant. I also admired his daring, his non-conformity."

A HAPPY BUT NUTTY SQUIRREL

During this period, Tex continued his nonconformist ways by developing a new character more insane than Daffy Duck, a rabid maniac with more than a few screws loose. His name was Screwy Squirrel. Originally created without a proper name, Tex's animators referred to him only as "the squirrel" until he was dubbed "Screwy."

An original 1943 revised model sheet of Tex's second MGM creation—simply dubbed by Tex's animators as "the squirrel"—who he ultimately called Screwy Squirrel.

Like Tex's earlier version of Warner Bros. Daffy Duck, the fuzzy-tailed Screwy was so off-the-charts that not even the frames of the film could contain his comical glee. He was the perfect Tex Avery creation: brash and erratic, and able to do almost anything at anytime. In the same way he broke conventions with Daffy by having him bound and "Who-hoo!" all over the landscape and the title cards in his first film appearance, *Porky's Duck Hunt* (1937), Tex defied all laws of science and logic with Screwy. He cast him as a misfit who destroys the perimeters of the cartoons he inhabits while revealing parts of the plot to the rest of the world.

On April 1, 1944, Screwy made his Technicolor movie debut in *Screwball Squirrel*. Screwy establishes his maniacal nature for audiences right away and throughout the film makes a mockery of the filmmaking process. In searching for nuts, the cackling squirrel provokes a mean-looking, peace-loving pedigreed bird dog, Meathead, who tries to catch the pestiferous squirrel who tortures him with everything he can find. After Meathead crawls through a hollow log and thinks he has lost Screwy for good, standing at the other end is none other than Screwy, holding a huge baseball bat. Not wasting a beat, Meathead says, "Duh, you're not going to hit me with that bat, are you?" Pausing, Screwy stares into the camera and says, "What do you think?" and then clobbers him.

MGM had high hopes for Screwy as Tex directed four *Screwy Squirrel* shorts within a year. That June, Screwy returned to the screen in his second short, *Happy-Go-Nutty* (1944), which is wilder and more frenetically violent than his first. This time "nuttier than a fruitcake" Screwy escapes from an insane asylum and provokes his favorite fall guy and institution's "Nut Catcher," Meathead, to chase after him. Screwy launches into commando mode and sets a bait of destructive traps that Meathead is too dumb to resist. He repeatedly tries returning the favor, chasing Screwy throughout the picture right past the "End" credits, prompting Screwy to remark, "Hey, that was the end of the picture." To which Meathead replies, "Yep, that's it all right," and then shows he's the "crazy" one by doing all sorts of comical gyrations before riding off on a toy hobbyhorse and crashing through the "End" credits frame.

Big Heel-Watha (1944), Screwy's third cartoon released that October, has Indians who are confronted by rationing trying to hunt for their food and being thwarted in their efforts—even by a skunk displaying a wartime rationing sign on its black-and-white striped tail that says: "No Ration Points Necessary." Tantalized in his quest to hunt for fresh meat by a big banner that reads, "Fresh Squirrel Meat Today," Big Chief Rain-in-the-Face (whose voice sounds like a slower version of Droopy) makes the mistake of tangling with nut-case Screwy, innocently reclining atop the doors to a small freezer. Screwy leaves a path of destruction in his wake, with the Chief as his primary victim. This nominal effort is mildly entertaining, despite its many gross racial stereotypes and characterizations of American Indians.

Tex departed from the delirium of Screwy to parody America's favorite pastime—baseball—in *Batty Baseball* (1944), released coinciding with the opening of the baseball season. Tex is spot-on comically exaggerating every aspect of the sport as the Yankee Doodlers play the Draft Dodgers at the W.C. Field. Referencing the wartime draft, the pitcher's uniform sports on the back the number "4-F" while other position players' uniforms are numbered "1-A." Even the characterizations are played for laughs, like a behemoth King Kong, pre-steroid-era sized player, with B-19 on his jersey, who dwarfs the catcher—and home plate—as he steps into the batter's box.

By January 1945, Screwy was back in his fourth MGM cartoon, *The Screwy Truant*. Once again, the wiseacre Screwy is paired with Meathead, this time playing a truant officer, who tries nabbing Screwy because he has skipped school and gone fishing.

Unfortunately, Tex was not able to exhibit Screwy's wild and brash humor in the way that endeared him to audiences. By now, the "chase" formula was beginning to wear thin, along with Screwy's grating laugh and over-the-top machinations to outwit—and pummel—his adversary. In essence, the character had become exceedingly contrived and obnoxious, but Tex did not give up on Screwy—not yet.

Tex's funniest shorts that year were his non-Screwy cartoons. One of his most outrageous romps marked the return of Happy Hound, now

One of Avery's memorable one-shot cartoons at MGM was his satirical look at the grand game of baseball, *Batty Baseball* (1944). *Courtesy Movie-Goods. © Metro-Goldwyn-Mayer.*

A scene from Screwy Squirrel's film debut, *Screwball Squirrel*, released in 1944. © *Metro-Goldwyn-Mayer.*

named Droopy, in *The Shooting of Dan McGoo* (originally titled, *The Shooting of Dan McScrew*), a spoof of the MGM feature *Dan McGrew*, distributed to theaters in March. This hilarious gag-fest casts Droopy as a "lone gambler" in a wild, rough Alaskan town, rich in gold and home to such major activities as "gambling, drinking, and shooting." Droopy's true love is the girl, Lou (played by Red—the same Red from *Red Hot Riding Hood*), and the stakes become high when the Wolf blows into town and falls for Lou and tries to drag her off. The short is layered with literal depictions of Robert W. Service's original poem, "The Shooting of Dan McGrew"—a character with "one foot in the grave" who walks up to the saloon bar, his tombstone and plot in tow, and the announcement of "the drinks are on the house," with the drinks suddenly taking a life of their own.

Unlike with Screwy Squirrel, whose out-of-this-world lunacy wore on audiences, Tex found in Droopy a character more steadfastly likeable and whose personality struck a chord with moviegoers. He featured the loveable hound in another short to round out the year, *Wild and Woolfy*. The film marked animator Walter Clinton's first as a new member of Tex's MGM cartoon unit.

Tex was contracted to make so many cartoons a year and Metro usually had a backlog of cartoons ready to be released. The 37-year-old veteran animator always had a backup plan in the event a story that he was developing for a future cartoon could not be resolved. He would revert to doing a cartoon based on a series of spot gags. His plan was not foolproof, however. Sometimes he would go ahead with directing cartoons that were "weaker ones," even when he could not resolve problems with the story. In an interview with author Joe Adamson, Tex cited *Car of Tomorrow*, one of his later satirical looks into the future, as one example: "That was one of those deals where we got stuck," he said, and he went ahead with making the cartoon anyway."

For Tex, his cartoons were all about the "finish"—developing a strong central idea or variations of a single gag that would build to a big laugh, a "topper" at the end. He relied usually on a simple idea that threaded everything together, and perfectly timed execution of the comedy and sight gags from start to finish. In a Tex Avery cartoon, timing was everything.

Tex lived to get a laugh and his sole purpose in doing animation was oriented toward entertaining himself as well as others. That year, he upped the ante by directing his second in a series of racy and risqué cartoons—displaying as writer Steve Schneider claimed "...a sexual frenzy that would have lowered Mickey's voice by several octaves"—by resurrecting his Red character from *Red Hot Riding Hood*. Once again he tested the moral guardians of the Hays Office to entertain audiences with *Swing Shift Cinderella*.

Released that August, *Swing Shift Cinderella* is Tex's retelling of the Cinderella story. It is more amorous and more outrageous than the classic children's fairy tale, with animator Preston Blair's Red as Cinderella (Cindy) holding down two jobs: aircraft plant worker by day and torch singer at a local nightclub by night. Seeing Cindy perform unbelievably

Droopy tangles with the Wolf again, this time in a Western-themed romp, *Wild and Woolfy* (1945). *Courtesy MovieGoods.* © *Metro-Goldwyn-Mayer.*

Avery's second so-called exploration of technology in the future, *Car of Tomorrow* (1951). *Courtesy MovieGoods.* © *Metro-Goldwyn-Mayer.*

Producer Fred Quimby looks over Avery's shoulder as he draws Screwy Squirrel for an upcoming theatrical cartoon short.

excites the lustful, slick-dressing Wolfie (Tex's Wolf character) as she does everything in her power to elude his advances. Meanwhile, Cindy's Fairy Godmother (her Grandmother)—formerly crowned "Miss Repulsive of 1898"—applies her "dubious charm" to win Wolfie for her own.

In March 1946, Tex starred Screwy Squirrel in what would be his swan song, *Lonesome Lenny*. For the film, he pairs Screwy with a new character, a big dumb dog, Lenny (once again parodying Steinbeck's Lenny character), who underestimates his strength and whose owners buy him a caged "Crazy Squirrel" (Screwy) from the local pet shop for a companion. No doubt aware this would be Screwy's final film, Tex kills off the character, with his new pal Lenny crushing him to death, and tries playing the character's demise for laughs with Screwy holding up a sign as he lay motionless on the ground that reads: "Sad ending, isn't it?"

Poster art to the final Screwy Squirrel cartoon, *Lonesome Lenny* (1946). *Courtesy MovieGoods.* © *Metro-Goldwyn-Mayer.*

Tex's greatest character success at Metro was Droopy. One of his finest was *Northwest Hounded Police*, issued to theaters on April 3, 1946, with Droopy as a Canadian Mountie on the chase after the Wolf again. Once again Tex goes outside the perimeters of the frames of film with the Wolf running so fast that he skids past the sprockets of the film.

When Bill Thompson, the voice of Droopy in most of the cartoons, was occasionally unavailable, Tex would step in and record the dialogue himself, and audiences hardly could tell the difference. Tex also supplied the voice of Junior in the *George and Junior* cartoons and the infectious chuckle of the bulldog in *Bad Luck Blackie*.

Tex was a taskmaster when it came down to laying the voice tracks of the characters in his cartoons. He would do 20 or 30 takes for one

Droopy, as Sgt. McPoodle, makes the Wolf "fall to pieces" in his hilarious escape in a scene from Avery's 1946 MGM cartoon, *Northwest Hounded Police*. © *Metro-Goldwyn-Mayer*.

line of dialogue, and while many did not hear much difference between them, he would sit in the projection room at the studio and run those scenes of dialogue "over and over and over and over again." As Heck Allen commented, "Hell, I couldn't tell one from the other. But Tex would eventually pick one."

As a director, Daws Butler—who started doing voice work for Avery in 1949—found Tex to be "very picky" when it came to laying the voice tracks. As he recalled: "Tex was a marvelous guy to learn the business with. He was the first brilliant (director), I ever worked for, and he's such a fussy man. This was before they had tape, and everybody was afraid of wasting film, so he would rehearse me, until I wouldn't have any voice left. There would be yells—he loved yells. I don't know if I invented the gag, but he sure used it a lot, where the guy hits his thumb and runs over the hill and dale, into the distance, and goes 'YEOWW!' A yell is a yell, and I do pretty good yells, but he would have me do about eight of these, then he'd say, 'Gee, that's close.' Then he'd say, "Well, let's lay one down,' then we'd do one on the film. Then he would throw in a couple of himself, just for protection."

TWO GEMS IN A JAM

Two months after the release of *Northwest Hounded Police*, Tex unveiled a new cartoon tandem to replace Screwy: two bears named George and Junior, who parody the characters George and Lenny from the novel and film, *Of Mice and Men*. The slapstick duo was reminiscent of the classic movie comedy team Abbott and Costello. George is the exceptionally intelligent, overbearing straight man and half the size of his gargantuan not-so-bright partner, Junior, who always manages to spoil George's big plans.

Premiered for audiences in *Henpecked Hoboes* on October 26, 1946, George and Junior are two hungry hoboes who want a chicken dinner. George hatches the perfect plan to catch a barnyard hen—donning a "rooster suit"—only for Junior to wreck everything.

Even though the cartoon received only fair reviews, George and Junior returned to star in more one-reel subjects, *Red Hot Rangers* and *Hound Hunters*, in 1947, and finally, *Half-Pint Pygmy* in 1948, which

Avery's spin on the Pilgrims landing at Plymouth Rock and feasting on the first Thanksgiving turkey dinner culminated in the gag-filled romp, *Jerky Turkey* (1945). *Courtesy MovieGoods.* © *Metro-Goldwyn-Mayer.*

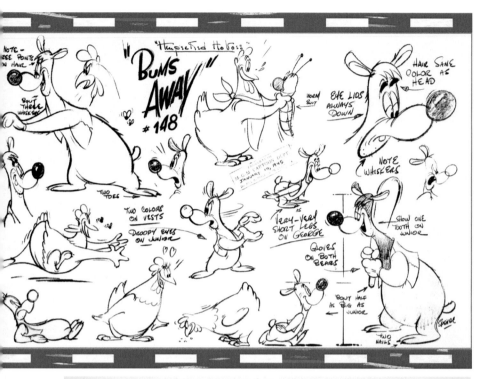

Once again parodying characters from John Steinbeck's famous novel *Of Mice and Men*, Tex created George and Junior, shown in this original model sheet from their first MGM cartoon, *Henpecked Hoboes* (1946).

received the series' worst reviews and resulted in the termination of the series.

In the meantime, Tex found joy in developing storylines and characters simply as a means to "bounce gags off" producing a series of one-shot, spot-gag cartoons, including *Jerky Turkey* (1945), *The Hick Chick* (1946), *Slap Happy Lion* (1947), *What Price Fleadom* (1948), *Little 'Tinker* (1948), *Lucky Ducky* (1948), and others.

Avery also turned his favorite, sexy and curvaceous star, Red, to appear in yet another sexual romp, *Uncle Tom's Cabaña*, which featured the work of a new member of Avery's unit, animator Robert Bentley. In this cartoon, issued to theaters in July 1947, Red turns up the heat on Little Eva. This happens after she hires a Disney-like Uncle Tom

Avery's sexy screen siren, Red, featured as a Southern belle who tries to save a plantation from being foreclosed on in Avery's forbidden master-piece, *Uncle Tom's Cabaña* (1947). Loosely based on the book, *Uncle Tom's Cabin*, the film has been censored from television due to its stereotyping of blacks.

(reminiscent of the character Uncle Remus from *Song of the South*) who tells the story to children of his attempt to save his land from foreclosure from the villainous Simon LeGree after turning his cabin into a nightclub. Dressed in stunning low-cut, off-the-shoulder layered white

Southern belle dress, Red provides the steamy hot entertainment. Singing a seductive version of "Carry Me Back to Old Virginny," she wows the patrons with her performance, her seductive beauty, and her sexy siren voice. When she appears to save the day, LeGree tries derailing Tom's efforts to keep his land but Tom "heroically stops him." Embellishing the telling of his story a bit—especially the "heroic" part—back in real time, Uncle Tom is suddenly struck by lightning. Due to the gross stereotypes and offensive characterization of the African-American Uncle Tom in the cartoon, the film is currently not shown on television.

Tex would bring Red back for a final encore in September 1949, in *Little Rural Riding Hood*, arguably the best of his Red/Wolf encounters with a more "cleaned up" yet beauteous Red—sleeker and more slender in her appearance. Red plays a big city girl and singer in this cartoon. The country boy Wolf's rich city cousin (voiced by Daws Butler in his first cartoon for Tex) invites him to see the "real" Red Riding Hood— after the Wolf falls for the plain-Jane Little Rural Red Riding Hood during a romp in the forest—and the country boy goes bananas when he sees Red. The city Wolf gets so fed up with his country cousin that he drives him back home. But when he does, he goes crazy over duller-than-a-doorknob Little Rural Red Riding Hood. The film reuses Preston Blair's animated song-and-dance sequence from *Swing Shift Cinderella* and marked Red's final screen appearance.

In 1948, Tex's unit underwent radical changes. After production of the last *George and Junior* cartoon, *Half-Pint Pygmy*, long-time story man Heck Allen was replaced by Rich Hogan starting with *Lucky Ducky*. He was later joined by co-collaborator Jack Cosgriff on many films. Many other animators joined the mix and changed hands from the late 1940s through the 1950s—Gil Turner, William Shull, Grant Simmons, Louie Schmitt, Michael Lah—along with two former colleagues, Bob Cannon (first credited on *Señor Droopy*) and Preston Blair (beginning with *Bad Luck Blackie*), and veteran Ray Patterson (his first being *Little Johnny Jet*).

During this period, three other shorts Tex directed rank as classics: *King-Size Canary* (1947), *Bad Luck Blackie* (1949), and *Ventriloquist Cat* (1950).

Mixing a cat, a canary, a dog, and a mouse with Jumbo Gro results in comedy exploits of epic proportions in Avery's classic cartoon, *King-Size Canary* (1947). © *Metro-Goldwyn-Mayer.*

King-Size Canary, released in December 1947, concerns a cat, a mouse, a dog, and a canary and at first centers on the starving cat, who imagines a feast awaiting her after spotting a refrigerator in a nearby house. But she must pass by a sleeping bulldog, Atom, to feast upon what is behind the fridge door. The cartoon short has the usual Avery spot gags, such as when the famished feline pries open a can of sardines, she finds only a sign that reads: "Kilroy Was Here." After the resulting chase, the cat discovers an even greater prize: a caged canary, the size of a thimble, and who clatters on the plate when the cat tries to eat her because she is so small and musters the remark, "Well…I've been sick."

Determined to eat the bird yet, the cat stumbles across a bottle of Jumbo-Gro, a chemical plant food, and pours the elixir into the little bird, imagining a more substantial feast. The canary grows to epic proportions and so does the cat after she takes a swig, as does Atom the bulldog after he drinks the leftover potion. The result is a madcap chase to the end—cat chasing canary, dog chasing cat, and losing the Jumbo-Gro down the chimney, only for a meek little mouse to take a sip, become gargantuan, and join the chase until no more elixir is left and the mouse says to the camera: "Sorry folks, we ran out of stuff. Good night." The camera pulls back to show the cat and mouse waving as they stand erect on the planet Earth.

Tex's January 1949 Technicolor release, *Bad Luck Blackie*, is a switch from *King-Size Canary* in that it pokes fun at superstition. He makes fun of those ancient notions that black cats bring bad luck—not ordinary bad luck but the Tex Avery brand. The myth comes true, at least in this cartoon, when a maltreated kitten hires a black cat to defend him from a sadistic bulldog.

Tex remembers having problems in developing an ending. "One picture we didn't know how to end was *Bad Luck Blackie*. We built that picture so that it went from the bulldog getting hit by a flowerpot to the kitchen sink to a battleship. To sort of get a little humor into the thing we had Blackie run across the dog's path differently each time—once on tip-toe, once like a Russian dancer. This was a gag within a gag. Finally we couldn't think of anything else to drop on him. How do you end it? Well, you're obliged to come back to the hero at the end of a cartoon. So you pull a switch—the kitten turns nasty and laughs like the bulldog did all through the picture."

Equally hilarious is *Ventriloquist Cat*, released in May 1950. This Technicolor short features a cat that discovers a mouthpiece which allows him to throw his voice like a ventriloquist. With the device, he is able to play all sorts of unkindly tricks on Spike the bulldog. It gets to the point that Spike smartens up and attempts to catch the cat by playing his own game: He dresses like a female feline, swinging his hips and puckering his lips. The cat almost falls for him until he realizes it is none other than Spike. For the topper, the cat throws his voice and a gang of dogs jump all over Spike, thinking he is the female cat.

Avery pokes fun at the superstition that black cats bring bad luck in a cartoon considered among his best at MGM, *Bad Luck Blackie* (1949). *Courtesy MovieGoods.* © *Metro-Goldwyn-Mayer.*

Droopy is pitted opposite the Wolf in a bullfight contest in Avery's classic cartoon, *Señor Droopy* (1949). *Courtesy MovieGoods. © Metro-Goldwyn-Mayer.*

Starting in 1949, Tex cranked out new *Droopy* cartoons with greater rapidity after the demise of his *George and Junior* series. His pint-sized hound continued to thrive, paired with his favorite foil, the Wolf, in *Señor Droopy* (1949), in which the winner of a bullfight gets "anything he wants in all Mexico." This was the first official cartoon in the *Droopy* series; also first to use the "Droopy" name.

TEETERING ON THE BRINK

In the meantime, Tex found it increasingly difficult to maintain the delicate balance of his career and his personal life. In 1947, he became a father for the first time with the birth of a son, Tim, and two years later welcomed a daughter, Nancy, into the world. But his intense perfectionism and dedication in keeping up his work took a huge toll on his family and him. He devoted more time to furthering his career than to parenting his two children and eventually career pressures caught up with him. In the fall of 1950, Tex took a year's sabbatical.

Later discussing this period of his life and constant pressure in his career, he said, "When you're making theatrical cartoons, you're using a half million of somebody's big fat dollars every year. And you feel that you've got to give them something. If you make a weak one, you feel, my gosh, you're letting down the studio."

Tex told author Joe Adamson the reason for the yearlong layoff was because he "got too wrapped up in my work. I tried to do everything myself." As a result, he did more than what a director usually would do. He would rough out the whole cartoon frame by frame and to stay on schedule work many Saturdays and Sundays. Handling so much of the technical side of making the cartoons—the pans, and putting a character in a certain spot of a scene—"got too rough for me," Tex said.

Oscar-winning animator Dick Lundy, hired by Quimby in May 1950 after working at R.S. Wolf Productions and previously as a director for Walter Lantz and Walt Disney, took over Tex's existing unit of animators—Walt Clinton, Michael Lah, Grant Simmons, and the newest arrival Robert Bentley (and borrowing Ray Patterson from Hanna-Barbera's *Tom and Jerry* cartoons)—and story men Heck Allen and Jack Cosgriff. He directed one *Droopy* cartoon in 1952, *Caballero Droopy*, as well as several cartoons resurrecting the studio's lumbering but lovable Wallace Beery-inspired character Barney Bear, including *Busybody Bear* (1952) and *Barney's Hungry Cousin* (1953). Lundy remained on board for a year and half before departing.

Lundy had a different take on Tex's sudden departure. In a letter to writer Mark Mayerson, who authored an article on the history of the MGM cartoons for *The Velvet Light Trap* film journal in 1978, Lundy wrote: "Tex Avery and Quimby had a little squabble and Tex left. According to Quimby, Tex would not return. I also knew that Quimby had wanted to start a third unit for a long time. So I thought that even if Tex did come back, Quimby would have his 3rd unit. It didn't turn out that way."

When Tex returned to MGM in October 1951, the cartoons he would direct were more stylized. With theater owners cutting the percentage of profits studios earned from their short-subjects as a result of antitrust legislation that broke up the monopoly of studio-owned-and-operated theater chains and studios needing to cut costs to survive, the lush-color animated characters and realistic third-dimensional backgrounds to which Avery was accustomed gave way to a flatter and more streamlined look influenced by UPA's revolutionary style of animation that used comparably fewer cels to animate an entire short.

The use of this newfound technology is notable in the films Tex made at MGM during the 1950s, including his latest Droopy cartoons, *Dare-Devil Droopy* (1951), *Droopy's Good Deed* (1951), and *Droopy's Double Trouble* (1951), his assorted specialties, including *Cock-a-Doodle Dog* (1951) with Spike and *Symphony in Slang* (1951), and his so-called explorations of technology of the future, *Car of Tomorrow* (1951) and *TV of Tomorrow* (1953), follow-ups to his 1949 cartoon, *House of Tomorrow.*

Double Trouble is Tex's most inventive *Droopy* cartoon during this period. In this Technicolor cartoon, Droopy is cast as a footman who is advised by the butler, Mr. Theeves, to "locate a reliable person" to replace him while he goes on vacation and protect the property and allow *no* strangers on the premises. Theeves hires the only person Droopy can think of: his twin brother Drippy, a muscle-bound brute who nevertheless looks exactly like Droopy. The audience soon distin-

An original Droopy hand puppet from 1952 among early merchandise of Avery's creation licensed by MGM. © *Metro-Goldwyn-Mayer*.

guishes the difference in characters, though, when Drippy makes his entrance by crashing through the door. "That's my brother, he's strong!" Droopy proudly remarks.

Droopy befriends a hobo, Spike the Dog (now sporting an Irish brogue), who mooches a meal off him. Droopy invites Spike for dinner, but while waiting outside and tucking in his napkin, Spike gets a mouthful of Drippy who pops him in the chops and sends him on a free trip south. Bedlam reigns throughout the entire cartoon with Spike being welcomed by the good twin, Droopy, then brutalized by the bad twin, Drippy. When Spike finally sees the two together, his jaw drops, his eyes bulge out, he gasps, he slaps his face with his feet—and generally goes batty—as an ambulance hauls the hysterical bulldog away.

Among Tex's inspired modern technology lunacy, *TV of Tomorrow* is a standout effort depicting, as critic Ronnie Scheib writes, "the takeover of the suburban household by a small box and the reciprocal smaller-than-life domestication of the image." The film outrageously illustrates the experience of this new technology in the home and unlimited designs and uses for it: a set that deals cards; a keyhole-shaped Peeping Tom set; and, "for those who like to gamble on their channel," a slot-machine model.

Quimby remained his usually ambivalent self about Tex's work, not always appreciating the fullness of his comic genius. When Tex directed *Symphony in Slang*, an animated, literal interpretation of popular slang like "I was in a pickle" and "I went to pieces," released in June 1951, Quimby had, as Tex recalled, "a hell of time trying to understand that one." The cartoon was a departure from Tex's usual gag-filled antics and he purposely made the cartoon to do "something fresh." Later, he admitted that "we were practically the only ones that laugh" at the film, but he enjoyed escaping from the standard comedy formula of "chases" and "explosions" used in his cartoons.

DROOPING ALONG

Tex's output slackened considerably from 1952 to 1953. He directed only three cartoons each year compared to his usually contracted six films annually. His cartoons were generally on the mark, including his 1952 releases, *Magical Maestro*, *One Cab's Family*, and *Rock-a-Bye Bear*. Work was completed in May 1952 on model sheets to the *Droopy* cartoon, the Western takeoff, *Homesteader Droopy*, with production of the film finished and released nearly two years later. The story, by Heck Allen, has Droopy out West to stake his claim, with the usual interference from his adversary, the Wolf.

After 1953, Tex directed about a half-dozen more *Droopy* cartoons, including *The Three Little Pups* (1953), *Drag-A-Long Droopy* (1954), *Homesteader Droopy* (1954) *Dixieland Droopy* (1954), *Deputy Droopy* (1955), and seven other specialties, including his second Oscar-nominated MGM short, *Little Johnny Jet*, an aviation send-up with the peppy offspring of an out-of-work B-29 saving the day, released in April 1953.

Of Tex's new *Droopy* cartoons, *The Three Little Pups* and *Dixieland Droopy* are among his finest. *Pups*, his latest parody of *The Three Little Pigs*, arrived in theaters in December 1953. It teams Droopy with two other "brain-dead pups," his brothers Snoopy and Loopy. As in the classic children's story, Droopy, Snoopy, and Loopy do everything in their power to keep a wacky Southern wolf who is a dogcatcher (the character's first film appearance voiced by Daws Butler, who also supplies the voice of Droopy) from breaking into their home. In the film, the slow-talking wolf, reminiscent of Butler's later Huckleberry Hound characterization, takes the brunt of the violent humor while chasing the three pups, made famous by his droll and unexpected comeback line, "Pretty smart li'l dogs in there!"

As was the norm in Tex's film work, sometimes gags are never fully explained and when they are, it's done for comical effect, like when the wolf swallows the pups' television set and when it returns in the next scene, one of the pups says, "Now don't ask us how we got the set back!"

When Tex previewed the film, the unpredictable Quimby, upon watching the comical antics of the wolf, gushed, "Yes, them things are funny. Every time he opens his mouth, he gets a laugh."

By now, Tex learned that anytime he cast the Wolf in impossible and dangerous situations by having him react more sedately with some funny off-the-cuff line, it won over audiences and Quimby. Even MGM short-subject star Pete Smith, a close friend of Quimby's, told the famed MGM producer, "Boy! You save that voice. I don't care what character you put with it, but you got a funny voice there."

Avery explores in uncharacteristic fashion the machinations of a taxi cab family, including a rebellious young son who refuses to follow his father's occupation, in *One Cab's Family* (1952). *Courtesy MovieGoods.* © *Metro-Goldwyn-Mayer.*

In December 1954, Tex's humor was more offbeat in *Dixieland Droopy*. Set to Dixieland jazz, the cartoon features Droopy as John Pettybone, an inspired musician who lives in a city dump and whose single ambition is to lead a Dixieland Band in the Hollywood Bowl. What ensues is a series of comical situations of Droopy in his quest to fulfill that desire. Along the way he befriends a "Musical Fleas" act featuring "Pee-Wee Runt and his All-Flea Dixieland Band" and succeeds in playing at the Hollywood Bowl as a Dixieland conductor.

Feeling as though his work was becoming redundant after having mastered the art of screwball cartoons, Avery was burned out. Animator Michael Lah remembered Tex often saying, "I've done it all a hundred different ways. I'm burned out. I just don't think the stuff is funny anymore."

With studios downsizing production of short-subjects, including cartoons, MGM eliminated Tex's unit at the end of 1954, with Hanna and Barbera surviving in dual roles as directors and producers replacing Quimby, who retired.

Tex's last cartoon for the studio was *Cellbound*, codirected by Michael Lah and released on November 25, 1955, one year after Tex left MGM. After his departure, MGM released two more CinemaScope offerings he directed: *Millionaire Droopy* (1956), a remake of *Wags to Riches* (1949), and *Cat's Meow* (1957), this time a remake of *Ventriloquist Cat* (1949), each produced by Hanna and Barbera.

Tex believes he succeeded in some ways at Metro but not as fully in developing a really successful character. "I never did develop a character as good as Bugs Bunny," he said. "I think I came close with Droopy but never really succeeded like Bugs did in my opinion."

While in the short term his future looked bleak, Tex's career was far from over. Opportunity would come knocking sooner than he would think.

7

One Last Splash of Buffoonery

After he departed from Metro, Walter Lantz offered Tex a lucrative contract to work for his studio. Lantz, known for making deals with a simple handshake, suspended this long-standing tradition by awarding him a written seven-year contract to supervise animation and create new characters and direct his own series of cartoons, receiving a percentage of the profits on his cartoons in return. Like an excited child, he told Tex's former Warner Bros. colleague Michael Maltese, who also joined Lantz's studio, "You know who I'm getting? I'm getting the guy I've been trying to get for years…Tex Avery!"

Lantz's enthusiasm was no surprise. He had always admired Tex's talent and sense of absurdity and comic talent from his time as an animator on the studio's *Oswald* cartoons 18 years earlier. As Lantz said in an interview, "The thing about Avery is that he can write a cartoon, lay it out, and do the whole thing himself. And when he's finished, it's great. He just *knows* comedy."

Before hiring Tex, Lantz brought on board two of his former MGM animators, Grant Simmons and Ray Patterson, immediately paired on two cartoons, *Broadway Bow Wow* and *Dig That Dog*.

After working at a studio run by corporate suits, Tex welcomed the change and working in an atmosphere like that of the Lantz studio. It was more relaxed, and workers answered only to one man, Lantz, who unlike Tex's previous bosses had a keen sense of humor. As Tex put it, "He'd leave us alone until the storyboard was completed, and then he'd probably put a little something of his in there, or change a little something." Avery later said he went "a little offbeat" on Lantz during his time at the studio but that he "appreciated it."

Tex worked at Lantz's studio with a renewed vigor and level of excitement he hadn't felt in years. Finally he felt he would have the chance to see many undeveloped gags and story ideas that he had been waiting to use come to fruition, unlike with past associations where he had to fight, it seemed, to have his ideas realized.

FISHING FOR LAUGHS

Lantz put Tex in charge of the studio's *Chilly Willy* animated series. There was one *Chilly Willy* in 1953, but Tex in effect had as much to do with creating Chilly as he did with Bugs Bunny. Chilly was a silent penguin that in his quiet way was just as devious as Screwy Squirrel.

Tex's first *Chilly Willy* cartoon for Lantz was *I'm Cold*, released on November 29, 1954. Not one of his stronger Lantz cartoons, it has Chilly seeking shelter from the frigid plains of the North Pole. He eventually secures himself in a fur warehouse, but not before he meets a watchdog whose delinquency is matched only by Chilly's ingenuity. That is when the chase begins. Overall, critics thought the cartoon "had its moments but not enough" to rank among Avery's best. He would follow this effort with a second *Chilly Willy* cartoon a year later, *The Legend of Rockabye Point* (1955), which was strong enough to be nominated for an Academy Award for "Best Short-Subject (Cartoon)" in 1956.

Tex worked hard to milk laughs out of Chilly, giving Lantz what he wanted, a cute penguin, and dreaming up comic foils with animator Paul Smith to play opposite of him—a dumb dog, seagull, or polar bear. But none of them worked because, as Tex said, "the penguin wasn't funny; there was nothing to it, no personality, no nothing."

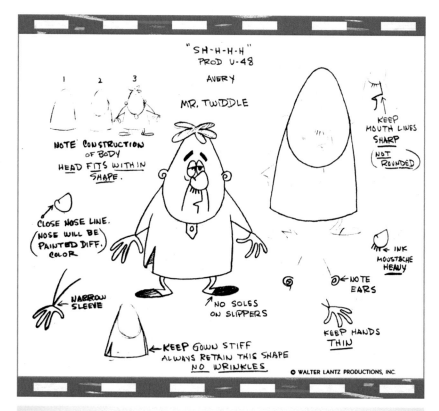

Character model sheet of Mr. Twiddle, a man seeking peace and quiet, from Avery's best film for Walter Lantz, *SH-H-H-H-H-H* (1955). © *Walter Lantz Productions.*

Meanwhile, Tex's output was far less than what he had done at Warner Bros. and MGM. He went on to direct two more lighthearted cartoon subjects: the *Walter Lantz Cartune Special, Crazy Mixed up Pup* (1954) and *SH-H-H-H-H-H* (1955).

SH-H-H-H-H-H is by far his funniest and most imaginative film endeavor under the Walter Lantz banner. The sparsely animated short, reminiscent in its design of the visually minimal UPA style of animation, stars a stressed out and overworked trumpet player, Mr. Twiddle, in desperate need of peace and quiet. Twiddle is told by his psychiatrist to visit the mountain retreat Hush Hush Lodge for the long rest he deserves. His silence is thwarted by a couple in the next room—a man playing a slide-trombone and a woman laughing hysterically to the point of being annoying. Mr. Twiddle bursts into their room, only to find that the cackling couple is his psychiatrist and his nurse.

Tex named and based the cartoon on a long-lost comedy record of the 1920s produced under the Okeh Laughing Record label and originally recorded in Germany, featuring a tavern owner and his wife laughing infectiously, to which he acquired the rights. The record was made to be played at parties and induce listeners into hysterics. In the film, he used the actual soundtrack of the couple laughing as the psychiatrist and nurse. Tex talked Lantz into making the film but it took considerable convincing on his part. As he recalled, "We called in a paint and inker or something, and said, 'Hey, listen to this,' and sat there, didn't say a thing, and watched them." Once they started laughing, Lantz went along with the idea.

While he was grateful to Lantz for the tremendous opportunity, professionally, in a short amount of time, Tex found his return to the Lantz studio less than idyllic. The budgets were much smaller than those at Metro and previously Warner Bros., and the quality and craftsmanship by comparison, in Tex's view, was "pretty crappy." Lantz later claimed that Tex was such a loner and perfectionist that he fretted most of the time over how "things would turn out." To alleviate the problem, Lantz teamed up Tex with one of the best gag and story men in the business: Michael Maltese, Chuck Jones's former story man at Warner Bros. Though they had a good, working relationship at Warner Bros. in the 1940s, by 1954, putting them together was like oil and vinegar: They did not mix. Maltese would sketch out storyboards and give them to Tex, only to find later that Avery had replaced them with his own. Maltese found the situation unworkable and complained to Lantz and Tex.

Another issue was Tex's insistence on doing only *his* cartoons. Lantz wanted him to direct some *Woody Woodpecker* cartoons but Tex demurred. Instead, as Lantz commented later, "Every subject had to be different," because Tex got bored easily doing the same thing too often. "That's why I got him to do a couple of *Chilly Willys*. I said, 'Look, Tex, you've got to be practical; you can't just make a cartoon a one-shot deal. You've to create characters that people remember, so they have some licensee value. If it weren't for our licensees, we'd be out of business."

Lantz did not want Tex to leave. After hiring him, his cartoons produced much better reviews from critics, and Tex brought a different pace to his cartoons, a vast improvement over the usually slow cartoons made by Lantz before his arrival. "He'd do the same routine, one thing right after another, a carbon copy," Tex said of Lantz.

In many respects, Tex was his own worst enemy. Despite his inherent brilliance, he let his constant worrying get in the way to the point that he decided he wanted out of his contract. His main complaint was over the percentage deal of his contract. While he earned a percentage of each cartoon's box-office gross, what he didn't realize, which he learned after consulting with an attorney, was that his profit came off the bottom instead of the top. So after deductions, including production costs and publicity, he would reap a mere pittance. Tex later said if he had continued to work under this agreement it would have taken him two to three years before turning a profit.

Tex later admitted that after Metro left him "in the cold" and earning a paycheck every week throughout his 30 years in the business, he panicked and said, "My gosh, there's no check this week, what are you doing to do?"

As his friend and former MGM colleague Michael Lah noted, "The spark was still there, but it was hard to keep up."

Lantz was unhappy to see Tex leave, especially after giving him the type of deal he had never offered anyone before. "I made Tex a wonderful offer. [But] Tex was always interested in getting that paycheck every week. He wouldn't gamble. If Tex had gambled, he would have been a millionaire if he had stayed with me. I think it was one of the biggest mistakes Tex ever made."

Heartbroken, Lantz chose Alex Lovy, long a director at Walt Disney, to head up Tex's cartoon unit. Lovy immediately benefited from two *Chilly Willy* cartoons that Tex had storyboarded before his departure and that Lovy directed, *Room and Wrath* and *Hold That Rock*, both released in 1956.

TURNING TO TELEVISION

Tex took a much-needed break from the pressures and daily grind of the business until a new opportunity presented itself. Television had become a thriving medium, with commercials becoming "the coming thing." After Tex retired from theatrical cartoon-making in 1955, Lah steered him to Cascade Studios, a small Hollywood studio, with whom he joined forces and freelanced as a director of television commercials. It was the right opportunity at the right time for Tex. Commercials generally last 60 seconds. They were much quicker to make than a six-minute cartoon and Tex enjoyed making them because, as he stated, "you make 'em in two weeks and you're through!" He didn't have the intense pressure like he had when he was directing short-subjects. He could direct a commercial in a day, including timing, voicing it, and doing the animation, and three weeks later, see the results on film.

For Tex, working in the commercial world was wholly different from his days as a studio animator and director. Young advertising executives were often "unfamiliar" or "indifferent" to his previous accomplishments— not even realizing, when Tex was asked to direct a series of Kool-Aid commercials featuring Bugs Bunny, that he was in fact Bugs' creator. It was long after this that he "started making it clear just who created Bugs Bunny."

Nonetheless, Tex's commercial work featured his brand of extreme double takes and wild exaggeration in many successful ad campaigns for Raid insect spray (in which his animated cockroaches, doing Tex Avery–style takes like mice fleeing a ship, shout, "R-a-i-d!"), Cricket Lighter, and Bryan Paint, with his commercials being honored with many industry awards, including International Publicity Film Festival Awards in 1957, 1958, and 1959 for Calo Tiger ads, and a Television Commercials Council Award in 1960. Tex also created a series of Frito-Lay commercials starring the mustachioed hombre, the Frito Bandito, drawing fire from groups about his character being too racist.

Tex took such complaints personally, even those about his older cartoon shorts shown on television or at film festivals from people saying, as he recalled, "This guy Avery…He killed people!" Tex was puzzled by such criticism. "I was thinking of funny cartoons, and all of a sudden this guy calls me a killer."

By 1970, Tex's personal life hit bottom. He was arrested for drunk driving and was ordered to attend 10 Alcoholics Anonymous meetings as part of his sentence. His son Tim died tragically in January 1972 from a heroin overdose at the age of 24. Tex was shattered by the loss. Shortly thereafter, he and his wife, Patricia, divorced, and he moved into a small North Hollywood apartment while continuing his battle with alcoholism.

Throughout this period, Tex shunned the spotlight. He regularly turned down requests to appear in public at festivals and celebrations of his work, including a weeklong tribute by the Museum of Modern Art in New York, and an invitation by the city of Dallas to accept a key to the city. On November 21, 1974, Tex broke from protocol. He and his former Warner Bros. comrades Friz Freleng and Chuck Jones were each honored by the Hollywood chapter of the International Animated Film Society (ASIFA) with its annual Winsor McCay Lifetime Achievement Award. For the occasion, voice artist June Foray, who supplied vocal characterizations in *Car of Tomorrow* (1951) and *One Cab's Family* (1952), requested the aging director draw a caricature of himself to be published in the award ceremony brochure. Tex did more than that: He drew a model sheet of himself exhibiting his trademark sense of humor and exaggerated style, with different character poses of himself in action.

Foray sensed during her conversation with Tex that he had grown to be an introspective man of conflicted emotions. He had become resentful of how other directors had tried to copy his style, while deferring any praise for his film achievements to being "nothing" without his writer and friend Heck Allen.

Though Tex never made another cartoon, his old films were rebroadcast on more than 200 television markets worldwide, including British television, drawing praise from fans of all ages who admired the legendary director's work. Former Warner Bros. colleague Bob Clampett noted that in England, "next to Walt Disney, he has now become the best known cartoonist."

As a result, Tex received thousands of fan letters from around the world. Joe Adamson, who wrote *Tex Avery: King of Cartoons*, has said he does not believe Tex answered "a fan letter in his life. His fan mail was delivered to a specific office building which he used as a mailing

Avery from one of his rare public appearances in the 1970s.

address. Nobody was ever there to receive the mail. Tex would come by and pick it up, but I can't ever remember him answering a fan letter. Tex just wasn't that kind of person."

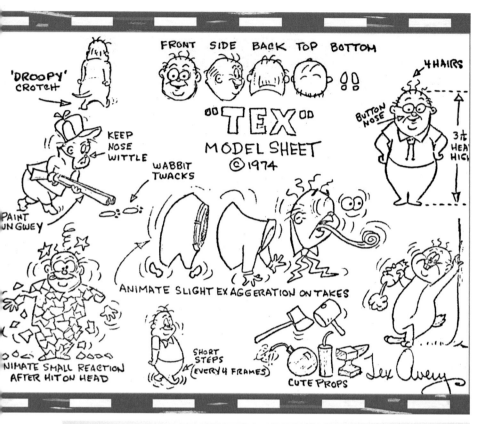

Avery mocks himself in assorted character poses in this self-drawn model sheet from 1974.

In 1976, Tex made a rare public appearance, accepting the invitation of UCLA's chair of animation Dan McLaughlin to attend a special screening of his cartoon shorts jam-packed with fans and students. The seemingly modest and gracious animator reminisced about his career, but in McLaughlin's words, Tex was "not too happy, low-keyed, genial, but beaten down." Tex was farther along in his recovery from drinking, having finally stopped.

Around 1978, Cascade Studios shut down its cartoon commercials division and Tex tried producing commercials with Bern Wolf, a veteran Disney animator. Nothing resulted from his efforts.

Afterward, Tex received job offers from old cartoon associates like Friz Freleng, who wanted Avery to help write Saturday morning cartoons. But he was not interested. He did have a change of heart about a year later, in 1979, when Hanna-Barbera Productions offered him a part-time job as a story man and gagman. To make him feel at home, the other animators hung a sign on the door to his office—coinhabited by veteran animator Chuck Couch—which read, "Welcome to Sun City." Tex found a renewed spark working with the studio's young animators where he was revered and treated like the legend he was.

Though in a much frailer condition, just like his days at Warner Bros., MGM, and Walter Lantz, Tex designed his own storyboards and model sheets and was responsible for editing stories and adding new gags. He never shied away from providing constructive criticism to his animators if he felt a gag they submitted needed improvement.

Tex worked on two series at Hanna-Barbera Productions, both of which saw network distribution. His first was a cartoon segment called, "Dino and Cavemouse," which aired as part of *The Flintstone Comedy Show* (1980–81).

Meanwhile, he also prepared a short pilot film for his latest creation, Kwicky Koala, an adorable, slow-moving, slow-talking but sly koala bear modeled after his famous MGM bloodhound, Droopy, who goes to great lengths to elude the grasp of his pursuer, Wilfred Wolf. The series was originally to be produced by special arrangement with a Canadian company and then be

Avery's final cartoon character creation, Kwicky Koala, made its television debut after his death. © *Hanna-Barbera Productions.*

Avery speaks at the 1977 Annie Awards at the Sportsmen's Lodge in Studio City, California. *Courtesy Raymond Cox.*

syndicated in the United States, to avoid some network restrictions. The pilot never sold.

Studio president Joseph Barbera praised Tex's work at the time, saying his "timing was wonderful. He was faster than the eye."

Tex's Kwicky Koala character was eventually packaged and sold to CBS with other cartoon shorts as part of the rotation under the name of *The Kwicky Koala Show* that would debut in the fall of 1981. Unfortunately, Tex never witnessed the fruits of his labor as this would become his final mark on the cartoon world.

Despite the support of former MGM studio rivals Hanna and Barbera and working in an environment where was valued and accepted,

Tex felt out of place in the current state of animation and increasingly frustrated and not terribly proud of his work, while battling cancer for the last year of his life.

After suddenly collapsing one day at the studio, Tex was rushed to St. Joseph Medical Center in nearby Burbank. Shortly thereafter, on August 26, 1980, he was pronounced dead of lung cancer. Eulogies poured in from many of his former colleagues and friends, including William Hanna and Joseph Barbera, Friz Freleng, Chuck Jones, Bob Clampett, and Walter Lantz, who lauded the veteran filmmaker for his decades of achievements and legacy of his work, leaving the world of animation better off for having known him.

Following Tex's passing, Lantz remarked: "Tex was a one-man deal. He was just great. He had some problems working with writers, because they couldn't savvy his style of humor. But if Tex wanted, he could do it all himself. He was just one of the greats in our industry. I can't praise Tex too much."

From creating so many unforgettable cartoons and characters to bringing unrestrained howls of laughter from audiences around the world, Tex Avery is one legendary master of screwball animation who expanded the limits of humor and animation like no other. For that, his legacy will live on in the body of his work, and the influence he continues to have on others.

SELECTED RESOURCES

For further study of Tex Avery's work and career, the following resources are recommended.

FILMOGRAPHY

Tex Avery (http://www.imdb.com/name/nm0000813/)

This site provides a complete list of every film and television production as animated and directed by Tex Avery.

DVD & HOME VIDEO COLLECTIONS

Bugs Bunny: Superstar (MGM Home Video, 1992)

Documentary produced in 1975 about Warner Bros. cartoon animation featuring interviews with legendary animators/directors Bob Clampett, Tex Avery, and Friz Freleng, as well as nine classic cartoons, among them, Avery's *A Wild Hare* (1940), the first official Bugs Bunny cartoon.

Daffy Duck: The Nuttiness Continues: Warner Bros. Golden Jubilee 24 Karat Collection (Warner Home Video, 1985)

Features eight fully-animated Warner Bros. Daffy Duck cartoons, including Tex Avery's *Porky's Duck Hunt* (1937), starring Porky Pig and Daffy Duck.

Looney Tunes Collector's Edition: Tex-Book Looney (Warner Home Video/Columbia House Video Library, 1999)

This DVD collection contains a dozen classic Warner Bros. cartoons directed by Tex Avery: *The Heckling Hare*, starring Bugs Bunny; *Daffy Duck in Hollywood*; *Dangerous Dan McFoo*; *The Blow Out*, featuring Porky Pig; *The Cagey Canary*, with Bob Clampett's pre-Sylvester and Tweety; *The Crackpot Quail*, with Bugs Bunny; *The Bear's Tale*; *The Haunted Mouse*; *Holiday Highlights*; *Egghead Rides Again*; *Hollywood Steps Out*; and *Tortoise Beats Hare*, starring Bugs Bunny.

Looney Tunes Golden Collection: Volume 2 (Warner Home Video, 2004)

Two-disc set of classic Warner Bros. cartoons by Tex Avery and others, including on Disc One the bonus feature, *Behind the Toons: A Conversation with Tex Avery*, a vintage interview with the late, great director.

Tex Avery's Droopy—The Complete Theatrical Collection (Warner Home Video, DVD, 2007)

Two-disc collection offering all 18 Tex Avery–directed *Droopy* cartoon shorts, as well as five by animator/director Michael Lah.

Tex Avery's Screwball Classics (1943) (MGM/UA Home Video, 1988)

First of three volumes on VHS featuring eight classic cartoons by Tex Avery: *Little 'Tinker, Swing Shift Cinderella, Magical Maestro, Bad Luck Blackie, Lucky Ducky, The Cat That Hated People, Symphony in Slang*, and *Who Killed Who?*

Tex Avery's Screwball Classics 2 (1946) (MGM/UA Home Video, 1989)

Collection of vintage cartoons directed by Tex Avery, including *Red Hot Riding Hood, One Ham's Family, Happy-Go-Nutty, Slap Happy Lion, Wild and Woolfy, Ventriloquist Cat, Big Heel-Watha*, and *Northwest Hounded Police*.

Tex Avery's Screwball Classics 3 (1945) (MGM/UA Home Video, 1991)

Contains six classic Tex Avery cartoons: *The Screwy Truant, House of Tomorrow, Flea Circus, Hound Hunters, Batty Baseball,* and *TV of Tomorrow.*

SELECTED BIBLIOGRAPHY

Adamson, Joe. *Tex Avery: King of Cartoons*. Cambridge, Mass.: Da Capo Press, 1985.

———. *The Walter Lantz Story with Woody Woodpecker and Friends*. New York: G.P. Putnam's Sons, 1985.

Beck, Jerry, and Will Friedwald. *Looney Tunes and Merrie Melodies: A Complete Illustrated Guide to the Warner Bros. Cartoons*. New York: Henry Holt & Co., 1989.

Blanc, Mel, and Philip Bashe. *That's Not All Folks!: My Life in the Golden Age of Cartoons and Radio*. New York: Warner Books, Inc., 1989.

The Boys from Termite Terrace. TV documentary, CBS, 1975.

Canemaker, John. *Tex Avery: The MGM Years, 1942–1955*. Atlanta: Turner Publishing, 1996.

Folkart, Burt. "Breeder of This Bunny Gave 'What's Up, Doc?' to World." *Los Angeles Times*, September 1, 1980.

Ford, Greg. "Tex Avery: Arch-Radicalizer of the Hollywood Cartoon." *Bright Lights Film Journal*, 64 (May 2009).

Guillot, Dorothy. "Stars of the Animateds and How They Grow." *The Dallas Morning News*, April 2, 1933.

Holberman, J. "Welcome to the Manic Kingdom." *Village Voice*, July 13, 1978.

Jones, Chuck. "Farewell to a Genius of Funny." *Los Angeles Times*, August 31, 1980.

Lah, Michael, interview. *Tex Avery*. TV documentary, Turner Broadcasting/Moondance, 1988.

Lenburg, Jeff. *The Encyclopedia of Animated Cartoons, Third Edition*. New York: Facts on File, 2009.

Lenburg, Jeff. *The Great Cartoon Directors*. Cambridge, Mass.: Da Capo Press, 1993.

Maltin, Leonard. *Of Mice and Magic: A History of American Animated Cartoons*. New York: Plume, 1987.

Mayerson, Mark. "A Letter from Dick Lundy." Mayerson on Animation. Available online. URL: http://mayersononanimation.blogspot.com/2006/05/letter-from-dick-lundy.html. Posted May 18, 2006.

Peary, Gerald, and Danny Peary, eds. *The American Animated Cartoon: A Critical Anthology*. New York: E.P. Dutton, 1980.

Schneider, Steve. *That's All Folks!: The Art of Warner Bros. Animation*. New York: Barnes & Noble, 1999.

Sennett, Ted. *The Art of Hanna-Barbera: Fifty Years of Creativity*. New York: Viking Studio Books, 1989.

Shull, Michael S., and David E. Wilt. *Doing Their Bit: Wartime American Animated Short Films, 1939–1945*. Jefferson, N.C.: McFarland & Company, 2004.

INDEX

ABOUT THE AUTHOR

Jeff Lenburg is an award-winning author, celebrity biographer, and nationally acknowledged expert on animated cartoons who has spent nearly three decades researching and writing about this lively art. He has written nearly 30 books—including such acclaimed histories of animation as *Who's Who in Animated Cartoons*, *The Great Cartoon Directors*, and four previous encyclopedias of animated cartoons. His books have been nominated for several awards, including the American Library Association's "Best Non-Fiction Award" and the Evangelical Christian Publishers Association's Gold Medallion Award for "Best Autobiography/ Biography." He lives in Arizona.

Photo courtesy: Brian Maurer